Heal Your Investments

A Story Your Banker Will Never Tell You

Heal Your Investments

A Story Your Banker Will Never Tell You

Alexandre Arnbäck and Trevor Pavitt

Translated by Rose Vekony and William Rodarmor

www.healyourinvestments.com

Printed in the United States of America

Second English Edition

ISBN-13: 978-1463659257

ISBN-10: 1463659253

Library of Congress Control Number 2011911317

CreateSpace, North Charleston, SC

For more information visit www.healyourinvestments.com

"If you're investing your savings in financial markets, you should read this entertaining and easily understandable book as soon as possible."
Spiros Mylonopoulos
CEO, Bergendahl & Son AB

"This book highlights the fundamental weaknesses of what is offered by banks and asset managers. It also shows an alternative that can be simple and attractive for many"
Icke Hamilton
Senior Advisor, Erik Penser Bank

"The authors have perfectly succeeded to explain why your investment manager is not an "advisor", rather a salesman who wants you to pay high fees for "advice" that has no expected added value."
Harry Flam
Professor of International Economics, Stockholm University

"I very much enjoyed reading this book, all the more so because the style is clear, incisive and educational. This book made a convincing case for rejecting the traditional management approach of invoicing fees that condemn you to net returns well below the market."
Frédéric Poulon
Professor at University of Bordeaux

"Heal your investments seems to me a work that is full of wisdom, explaining in a very instructive way what is at stake in portfolio management. During turbulent times (or the current gloomy times), it's a book that is right on target."
Pierre de Senarclens
Professor at University of Lausanne

"Comparing with a metaphor of the book: In a dark room a child is afraid to the unknown thing. The authors put in investors hands who are afraid of the darkness of the unknown thing, a lantern to illuminate

and to help them discover what is really in the room, dissipating ghosts and siren's songs with fundaments and principles that nobody must ignore."

Pedro Sepúlveda Gutiérrez
Director of Finance Programme for Directors,
Executive Education, ESADE Business School

"This book is a fast, easy read for both the innocent novice and more experienced investor. Clearly extensively researched with quotes from Adam Smith (1776) right up to DSK's misjudgements (... the financial ones!) with the wisdom of numerous Nobel Prize winners thrown in for good measure. The Technical Notes section at the end is particularly interesting. If you read this the book the pompous banker will surely squirm in his/her seat when next you meet. For this reason alone it's worth the $20 investment. I would heartily recommend this book to anyone with a bit of money right up to the mega-rich."

Robin Morris
Comment on Amazon.com

"A book that is accessible to everyone. Even those without financial expertise will very quickly understand the subject. The book is very well structured; kudos to the two authors for all their research work, which allowed them to explain sometimes complex procedures simply and clearly."

Serge Guinand
UBS

"I found this book fascinating and very instructive. The authors deserve a round of applause for having had the courage to confront certain taboos through knowledge and information."

Rémy Baddour
Insurance broker

"After only a few hours of reading, the sometimes opaque systems employed by banks suddenly become clear and comprehensible. The authors lead you, step by step, using very concrete examples taken from everyday life, to understand how a bank functions, and they don't hesitate to touch on sensitive points. This book may not make you more intelligent, but it will certainly keep you from being duped!"

A banking lawyer

"Really, this is a simple work, one that is accessible to anyone; it's true, precise and intended for all managers... I only wish that they would keep it at their bedsides to consult it and learn from it, especially considering that it is HIGH time to admit that clients cannot keep being the cash cows for a system that is corrupt and opaque, even obsolete! Thanks to both of you for this honest and topical account."

Alexandre de Pierpont
Advisor

"Whatever his position in the debate between passive and active management, and whatever his opinion on the practices of wealth management, the reader cannot ignore the facts brought to light by this book."

Christian Mustad
Partner, Edgar Brandt Advisory

"At a time when it is essential to separate the wheat from the chaff, when regulation is heavy-handed and a battle of interests ensue, there are some financiers willing to define positive practices. That's true of these bankers/authors who offer investors a method of investing known as "passive" investment. This is truly an intelligent and rational strategy, and one solely in the client's interest. "

Denis Dupré
Professor of Finance and Ethics
Holder of the Responsible Managers Chair, University of Grenoble

Contents

Preface

Let's start with the bad news: in finance, there is no miraculous formula for success. It's a reality that may be hard to swallow, dashing the hopes of millions of investors. But at an unconscious level, everyone knows it's true.

Nonetheless, the alchemy of finance still stirs our desire for prodigious wonders. Financial specialists—bankers and wealth managers—seem like wizards whose often contradictory counsel is delivered in a complex, obscure jargon, difficult for the uninitiated to understand. How, then, are we supposed to choose from among the impressive array of financial strategies and products? And above all, how will we find the investment style that is right for us?

This book will answer all these questions and offer concrete solutions.

It attempts to allay common fears about the process, first by explaining the investor's anxiety and then by providing keys to understanding the finance industry. Armed with a clear notion of how the market works and who the different players are, you will be able to grasp the main aspects of the industry. All it takes is a willingness to look at finance in a new way and sharpen your critical judgment.

Our understanding of society allows us to form our own opinions about politics or medicine or food. Shouldn't it be the same with regard to finance, which, after all, has such a great impact on our lives?

By following common sense, bolstered by facts, we arrive at a new investment approach, one that offers both peace of mind and excellent returns.

Passive management has been around for more than forty years; today it's the method used to manage 15% of the world's wealth. In the following pages we will present the mechanisms and the advantages of this type of management, and explain why its popularity is growing among private investors.

Between them, the authors Trevor Pavitt and Alexandre Arnbäck have more than thirty-five years' experience in finance, Pavitt having worked in several large international banks and Arnbäck in a private Swiss bank. Like many other bankers, they witnessed their clients' anguish and the conflicts of interest inherent in their jobs. In response to these problems, they turned toward a type of management that affords both mental and financial peace of mind.

Through this accessible book, based on their concrete experience and careful research, they offer investors the tools to help them take back the reins of their own finances. As we shall see, it's a simple and straightforward—hardly magical—approach.

Money and Stress

Why is money such a source of stress? It's perfectly understandable to be anxious when you don't have enough money to take care of your own needs or your family's. But why do people who *do* have enough and who have put it in the bank—a presumably safe place—also worry about money?

Do only certain groups of people experience this stress? Does it have something to do with age, gender, or social class? Whether one is retired or actively employed, thrifty or a big spender, knowledgeable about finance or a perfect novice? If you think about it, none of these factors can explain the investor's anguish. Even the amount of money doesn't make a difference: millionaires, those on a comfortable salary, and those with a modest income all share this fear of loss. Whether we're talking about $100 million or $100,000, it's the same story. The risk of losing even 5% is hard to put into perspective, and can sometimes make it hard to sleep at night.

Anyone who has savings is exposed at one time or another to the risk of loss.[1] Of course, that doesn't mean that having money is the problem. Rather, the problem is how to manage that money.

Who wasn't alarmed, or at least concerned, by the rumors that UBS would go bankrupt in Switzerland,[2] or by the Kerviel/Société Générale affair in France,[3] or by the world economic crisis in 2008? The finance pages are filled with these stories of great banking institutions that,

---

1   National Survey by the American Psychological Association (APA), International survey by Reader's Digest in 2006, Study by the University of Cambridge, 2008.
2
− Zurichers say "UBS won't go bankrupt like Swissair." *www.bloomberg.com*, 02.10.2008.
− Frédéric Goujon. "Et si UBS faisait faillite?" Toutes Taxes Comprises (Swiss television series, TSR 1), 09.03.2009.
3   Claire Gatinois and Anne Michel. "Société Générale: six questions sur une fraude." *Le Monde*, 26.01.2008.

though armed with the best specialists, lost billions of dollars overnight. In the face of such collapses, it's normal to fear for one's own investments, no matter what money managers tell us. You remind yourself of your banker's reassuring words, the good or bad news he judiciously explains; he seems to be on top of the situation. Nonetheless, the anxiety's still there.

A simple analogy might explain why.

Between ages two and five, children are often afraid of the dark. In the darkness, they find themselves completely disoriented, unable to recall the layout of their room. Which way is the bed facing? And where is the lamp, the door? They lose control of their environment, and no matter how much their parents may have reassured them while tucking them into bed, they start to panic.

Investors know the feeling. For them, the darkness is the uncertainty surrounding their investments. They may trust their banker implicitly and listen to all the detailed explanations justifying every rise or fall in their stocks, but they still don't quite grasp the ins and outs of their investments.

"Your shares have gone up, just as I thought they would, because all the indicators were favorable." Or, conversely, "Your shares have gone down because there was simply no way to foresee such-and-such event, which is what triggered the loss." Both scenarios seem to hinge on the banker's shrewd analysis of current conditions. But in reality, each outcome essentially relies on prediction. And since no one can predict the future—not even the most brilliant economists or the most profitable bankers—this great unknown harbors darkness and stress.

Another disorienting factor is the difficulty in assessing the impact of a gain—but especially of a loss—on one's overall portfolio. Just as a child can no longer locate the familiar reference points (the bed, the lamp, the door) in the darkness, so too the investor, given the murky view of his investments, is unsure how to interpret his losses in terms of real life. Does the loss equal a month of vacation? His youngest child's education? The early retirement he has dreamed about? If you were to find that you had lost, for example, 25% of your assets, what would this number mean to you in real life? The important thing isn't knowing why the banker's prediction proved right or not, but rather knowing the actual impact of this loss. After all, the investor's worries aren't about numbers or percentages, but about what the money corresponding to those figures would allow him to do—or not do.

The darkened room stirs the child's imagination and unleashes all sorts of fears. As his inability to grasp his surroundings grows, his interpretation of shapes and noises becomes less and less rational, until finally, convinced that the room is full of monsters and witches, he bursts out crying. Likewise, when the investor has no clear view of his financial situation, he falls prey to doubts that distort his judgment and lead him to make poor decisions.

Take the example of Swissair, the prestigious airline that went bankrupt in 2002. Imagine that you had stock in the company when the first rumors began to circulate, a few weeks before the bankruptcy. You suddenly realize that your shares have lost half their value. What should you do?

Your banker had advised you to put your money in Swissair, but he was wrong. No matter how sound his analysis may have been, it was still based on prediction. You begin to have doubts. If this professional can make such a mistake, how can you continue to trust him? And if you can't trust him, whom can you trust?

To decide on your next move, you try to interpret whatever information is available. Some newspapers insist that the Swiss government will never let its flagship business go bankrupt. So should you do nothing, because the company will be saved by the government, and its stocks will surely go back up someday? Should you, in fact, buy more shares, convinced that this is the only way to recoup your loss? Or are you going to sell everything so that you don't lose any more?

Besieged by such doubts, and having neither the information nor the tools to respond sensibly, investors have acted irrationally. They have followed that little voice in their heads that conjures up monsters hidden in the dark. They have let themselves be guided by vague intuitions, manipulated by growing stress—that is, by their emotions. And it's rarely advantageous, in any area of life, to get carried away by emotions. Doubt and the sense of urgency lead us straight into errors of judgment.

Rather, the best way to respond in a time of crisis is to take action on the things we can control. In our example of Swissair, the investor should have asked himself, "At what point does a loss start to threaten my plans?" This simple calculation is in itself a good barometer. Identifying and setting limits enables us to determine the rules by which to act. This way, we take charge of the things within our control.

When your banker asserts, "That particular product is riskier; you may have greater gains but also greater losses," do you have a clear notion of that risk? Do you know how much you could allow yourself to lose? That is where the danger lies—where your own "monster," the source of your stress, is lurking. Because the mistake isn't risking money; it's not having established beforehand the amounts you are prepared to put down...and prepared to part with.

Taking Back Control

You need to get to the root of the problem in order to solve it. There are simple steps you can follow, as well as effective tools for regaining your peace of mind.

Remember, the grown-ups' reassuring words aren't enough to help a child overcome his fear of darkness. Instead, guided by his parents, he has to find the resources within himself.

In the same way, as an investor, you take the first step of deciding to take back control of your finances. After all, no one is better placed than you to look out for your own interests. This doesn't mean you should pull all your money out of the bank. Instead, you need to take back the reins over your investments and let your banker know how to work for you. Investors need to realize that bankers serve their shareholders as well, and often put those interests ahead of their clients' interests.

Just as the child's fears dissipate when the light is turned on, revealing the true contours of his room, so the investor must illuminate his own goals—the wants and needs associated with the future use of his investments. This means establishing a concrete plan, a list of the things you wish to accomplish in the years to come. Such a plan outlines the general direction toward which your investments should be oriented, while also setting your tolerance for risk.

Now that the spaces he found so terrifying in the dark are all lit up, the child reclaims his room and regains a sense of control. The same process operates when the investor establishes his plan: he determines reference points that will enable him to act rationally, rather than merely react emotionally, in moments of crisis.

When you take the lead by giving your own investment directives to your banker, it is crucial to observe one rule: make sure you only invest knowledgeably, putting your money in simple and robust investments whose workings you fully understand.

By way of illustration, remember the Bernie Madoff affair. All the investors who were swindled—from the most seasoned financiers to the least experienced neophyte—had one thing in common: none of them understood what Madoff's miraculous formula actually consisted of. And had they understood, the scheme would never have worked.[4]

Finally, to reassure their child, his parents place a night-light by the bed. Once you have established your plan and given your directives to invest in products that you understand, your safety net—your "night-light"—will consist of checking on your investments a few times a year, to make sure that your banker is following your plan.

The combination of these simple precepts will enable you to overcome any anxiety about your investments. To achieve the impact of this method on your personal situation, you will need objective knowledge of how the market works, as well as the ins and outs of wealth management. Let's "turn on the light" now to examine the colossal machine of financial markets and the main aspects of traditional management.

---

4   Sylvain Cypel. "Comment 'Bernie' les a tous bernés." *Le Monde*, 16.12.2008.

Illustration dem
light shining!
on "TRADITION
MANAGEMENT"

• • • •

This book is divided into three parts.

In the first part, we will look at the mechanisms of the finance industry, noting its flaws and how they affect traditional wealth management, called **active management.**

In the second part, we will find out how to get around these difficulties by taking a different approach, **passive management,** which relies on facts and eliminates the stress that can come with investing.

Finally, for those who would like more detailed explanations of the various subjects discussed in the first two parts, technical notes follow at the end of the book.

Part I:
Shedding Light on the Finance Industry and Its Flaws

1.
Fresh Cod or Nestlé:
The Story Is the Same

The Laws of Supply and Demand

As confusing as financial markets may seem, the system actually isn't that complex. The way it works is relatively simple: the market is a place where sellers and buyers meet in order to carry out a transaction. On the one hand, businesses in need of financing offer investors the opportunity to invest in their potential to earn more than the initial outlay. On the other hand, investors seek out the best stocks, or the businesses with the most potential, in order to grow their money.

The financial market is an arena of exchange much like any other. For instance, let's imagine you go to a fish market. As you enter, you're greeted by the smell of fresh fish. You see the many stands occupied by fishermen and fish merchants, each one trying to get the best price for the day's catch. And you hear the hubbub of the families and restaurant buyers who have come looking for the freshest fish at the lowest cost.

The vendor is free to set whatever price he chooses for his fish. He must, however, take into account his clients' needs and budgetary constraints, as well as the prices being asked at the other stands. Whether cod or shares in Nestlé are for sale, the market is a competitive realm. If one vendor decides to sell his fish at $10/lb. when the neighboring stands are selling the same thing at $5/lb., he runs the risk of not selling off the whole day's catch, and thus losing money.

A balanced price falls within a narrow margin, somewhere between the price at which the seller agrees to sell and the buyer agrees to buy.[5] Just as the fisherman cannot lower the price beyond a certain point without losing money he needs to continue fishing, so too the buyer cannot, in view of his other needs, pay above an amount that exceeds his means. The problem is that both these limits are based on an infinite array of factors. Because of this, the fish market, like all areas of our lives, is not immune to sudden upheavals.

Perhaps an oil spill has wiped out the marine fauna. Or maybe a storm has kept all the fishing boats in port. Or perhaps it's become illegal to fish with nets. For hundreds of reasons that no one could foresee, the fisherman's catch could dwindle, and the market stalls would have less fish to sell. With just as many people wanting to buy, however, fresh fish would become a rare commodity, and the fishermen could then raise their prices.

> "The stock market is made up of lots of buyers and sellers who have access to the same information. If you think Microsoft is cheap at $29 a share, you're betting that you know something the trader selling it to you from Fidelity or Goldman Sachs or some hedge fund hasn't figured out."
>
> **Pat Regnier**
> **Journalist**

Just as supply affects the price, so too can demand. If for some reason the market is less busy from one day to the next, the fishermen have to sell their catch cheaply in order to minimize their loss.

The Financial Forecast

These market cycles, whether positive or negative, are impossible to predict. At the stock exchange, billions are paid each year to financial analysts who predict which stocks will rise and which will fall.[6] Their expertise draws on sophisticated studies. But can they anticipate an oil crisis, a country's bankruptcy, or a natural disaster? And not just national or world events influence the market rates. A human incident,

---

5   Alfred Marshall, *Principles of Economics,* 8th ed. New York : Cosimo Inc., 2009
6   Mark Hulbert. "Can you beat the Market? It's a $100 Billion Question." *New York Times*, 09.03.2008.

however frivolous it might be, can also have formidable repercussions. In 1998, the Dow Jones industrial average dipped amid news of the Monica Lewinsky scandal at the White House, an intimate relationship between two adults.

Believe it or not, though inherently unpredictable, the human factor, and nature in general, are both crucial to finance. The market fluctuates in response to extremely varied parameters that change the prices of shares every day.[7]

Finance is not an exact science, though it's frequently made out to be—and this misconception generally benefits the financial industry. We let the specialists lead us on with their apparent logic underpinned by a wealth of figures and calculations that blind us to the fundamental nature of the financial world. Finance is a human and social science, with no mathematical precision. This essential characteristic makes any sort of forecast impossible. And if no one can know in advance the price of fish at the local market, how can anyone foresee prices of sprawling financial markets on an international scale?

We can be certain of two things:

- No one can predict the future.

- In finance, too, no one can predict the future.

---

7   "The price of any stock is unpredictable." Paul A. Samuelson. "Proof That Properly Anticipated Prices Fluctuate Randomly." Industrial Management Review 6:2 (1965): 41.

2.
The Schizophrenic Bank

Various actors play a part on the vast stage of the financial market. The different finance professions are hard to define and categorize. Let's look at the two main activities at a banking firm in order to better understand how a bank works.

The Bank as a Vault

A bank's primary function is to safeguard deposits, assuring the physical security of the money. In addition to this service, the bank provides other conveniences, such as accounting, transfers, checkbooks, credit cards, and loans to qualified individuals and businesses.

The people involved in these administrative and logistical operations can be categorized as back-office or operational staff—those in charge of carrying out the client's instructions.

At this level the bank's relationship with the client is generally clear and straightforward: the client fully understands the services the bank provides and the fees it charges for them.

From these basic operations the banker makes a decent living—but not any more than, say, a supermarket manager, whose chain sells the same types of products found at other chains, at similar prices. Because all banks offer deposit services, they need to remain competitive, which means that products and fees are generally comparable across the industry.

Everyone knows, however, that there is a big difference between a supermarket manager's salary and a wealth manager's. What allows a banker to make so much more?

The Casino Bank

In addition to their deposit services, banks have developed a new business: creating and selling financial products.

Here the banker becomes a bit like the radio announcer urging shoppers to check out the latest sales. A store often makes its biggest profit by promoting "great deals" to turn over its stock: "This weekend only, every household appliance is on sale! Trade in your old toaster oven, food processor, or coffeemaker for the latest model at deep discounts! But hurry—sale ends Sunday!"

Banks, too, promote their financial products, employing money managers, analysts, and advisors to buy and sell to their clients, who are like customers at a supermarket. It's not enough for them to fill their shopping carts with whatever is on their shopping list and head to the checkout line. Instead, special sales entice them to "save money" by buying more.

Bankers, too, have a whole arsenal of marketing ploys to sell their financial products. Guaranteed capital! Double-digit performance! Exceptional growth! Their "sensational" sales pitch abounds with such terms, discouraging critical thinking and distracting attention from the important questions: What exactly do these miracle products consist of? And, above all, do they answer an actual need? Keep in mind that the new funds created by the bank are made up of products that already existed. Apples sold by the piece have the same properties as apples on sale by the bag; the difference is that by choosing the bag, you end up buying more than you really need. Similarly, products that the bank offers are rarely adapted to the client's financial goals.

In the murkiness surrounding these investments, we're lured by the glittering promise of potential gains.

How can we know what really underlies the banker's choices in assembling a portfolio? How can we be sure he is choosing the best products, and not simply ones that will get him a higher commission? Obviously, for all these transactions, the banker is handsomely remunerated.[8] As we shall see in greater detail in the next chapter, the commission system is a veritable bonanza for the banking industry.

Thus, beyond their custody function, banks build their fortune on their clients' transactions. These clients get caught up in the market game and are persuaded to buy the bank's products. That is how the banking industry amasses millions, and how bankers collect their bonuses.

With the bank's sales function—its packaging of financial products—comes an elaborate operation aimed at influencing its clients' decisions. The better the "advisor" is at getting clients to buy and sell, the more transaction orders there are, and the more the bank and its bankers earn. So naturally they talk up the wonders of their product and the advantages it offers that their competitors can't match—all to spur further sales. We see the same trick with the store ad that emphasizes the sale's urgency as well as the extraordinary nature of its supposed "great deals."

Of course, the banker's advice is based on a real analysis of the markets. Behind the advisor and the offers he promotes are armies of analysts, brokers, traders, and the like, all working to track down and supply the most promising and attractive investments. To convince its clients to invest in China, for example, the bank first hires a team of specialists in charge of selecting the best Chinese companies. Next it has negotiators purchase the stocks. Then strategists and lawyers create the products. Finally, the bank's marketing people produce an enticing package to lure investors.[9] Thus, the bank's advisory function requires a tremendous amount of preliminary work—and, obviously, expense, because the experts in these various areas must all be paid.

8
- Jean-Claude Péclet. "Comment payer mon banquier?" *Le Temps*, 02.02.2009.
- Mark Hulbert. "Can you beat the Market? It's a $100 Billion Question." *New York Times*, 09.03.2008.
9 Take a look around you. It's very apparent that marketing is one of the banks' major expenses.

The Weak Spot[10]

The banker claims to contribute significant added value through his advice. His analysis is rigorous, and he is convinced that he is helping his client choose the best investment. After all he has privileged information the client doesn't have.

Let's not forget, however, how supply and demand can influence price fluctuation and market climate. Even though the banker may see himself in a neutral position between sellers (the companies offering their stock) and buyers (his clientele of investors), he is no less subject to the formidable risks inherent in financial affairs.

To illustrate the limits of the banker's role, let's slip on a dinner jacket or an evening gown and head to the casino.

The banker is like that acquaintance we run into at the roulette table. He tells us with conviction, "I've been watching the table for over an hour, and I've noted the other players' results—all the numbers and colors that have come up. If you want to win, bet on red." The patience of this observer (just like the banker and his analysis) may make his tip seem valuable, but the capricious little ball can just as easily land on black. So, yes, you can hit the jackpot, but you also risk losing all your chips.[11] In urging you to bet on red, our expert turns out to be right the first time. He offers more predictions, and we win the next two times as well. Does that mean he's "unbeatable" at roulette? That his knowledge, his gambling "skill," enables him

---

10   Standard & Poor's, Standard & Poor's Indices Versus Active Funds Scorecard, Year End 2008, www.spiva.standardandpoors.com, April 2009.

11   Past performance is no guarantee of future results:
– Christopher R. Balke and Matthew Morey. "Morningstar Ratings and Mutual Fund Performance." Fordham University's Graduate School of Business, 22.12.1999.
– Anna Robaton. "FRC Study Raps Morningstar Ratings: All-Star Battle Over Performance." Investment News, 29.03.1999.
– "Why Top Performance Is a Poor Indicator of Future Performance," report by Smith Barney Consulting Group, 1997.

to monitor the ball's results better than the other players? No, of course it doesn't.

Conclusion

In spite of their obvious limits, financial products never fail to fascinate. Latching onto this "enchantment," banks stimulate energy and enthusiasm without producing concrete value.[12]

Thus, the investor must know how to distinguish the bank's custody function from its financial advice (or sales) function. A provider of services and a promoter of dreams—these two poles of banking activity, though very different in nature, are all too often confused in the mind of the public. It's obviously very practical and even entirely necessary to make use of the bank's vault. But why give the banker the key?

> "Wall Street's favorite scam is pretending luck is skill."
>
> **Ron Ross**
> **Economist**

---

12   Berkshire Hathaway Inc., annual report, 2005.

3.
The Good, the Bad, and the Ugly: Advisors, Fees, and Conflicts of Interest

In most cases, the banker, in his role as an expert, advises the investor in good faith. If he wants to keep his clients, the banker has a vested interest in making their money grow, or at least in preventing losses. This tacit agreement between the banker and his client establishes a legitimate relationship of trust—except for one thing: fees. When your banker manages your portfolio, your money is subject to four types of fees, which few investors fully grasp.

The Management Fee

The management fee refers to the fee the manager charges to manage the investment account. Investors tend to focus on this initial expense and overlook subsequent ones in calculating the compensation the bank receives. After all, it's quite an imposing tree—but one that hides a lush forest![13] It is, of course, only logical to be charged a certain sum in exchange for a service. But the banking system, along with other money managers, doesn't stop there.

---

13   Brad M. Barber, Terrance Odean, and Lu Zheng. "Investors would benefit from a greater understanding and awareness of mutual fund expenses.... Expenses that remain out of sight are likely to remain out of mind." "Out of Sight, Out of Mind: The Effects of Expenses on Mutual Fund Flows," Journal of Business 78 (2005): 2095–2119.

The Transaction Fee

In addition to the management fee, the banker gets paid for each transaction. It's therefore in his interest to generate numerous transactions and step up the pace of buying and selling.

If the shares of Coca-Cola stock that he bought for your portfolio at $100 suddenly climb to $120, you're likely to hear, "We should cash in!! Let's sell Coca-Cola and buy Nestlé; those shares cost $90 and are sure to go up quickly." What that means, in concrete terms, is that your banker will have taken 1% on $100 (the purchase of Coca-Cola shares), 1% on $120 (the sale of that stock), and another 1% on $90 (the new purchase of Nestlé shares).

Now imagine the opposite scenario, back at the roulette table. Flush with adrenaline at his first loss, our expert rages, "Black?! What rotten luck!! But I'm sure of my probability calculations. Let's switch tactics and bet on the odd numbers; they haven't come up in over half an hour. Now's the perfect time."

If that expert were the banker, he'd take 1% to bet on red; another 1% to sell the red, even though it has lost value; and then 1% to bet on the odd numbers.[14]

In both cases, notwithstanding his good faith, the banker encourages further transactions, from which he always stands to profit. He is not entirely manipulative; when he wants to buy Nestlé or bet on odd numbers, his prediction is based on a solid analysis. Nonetheless, the investor must not forget the interest his bank has in constant

> "The house [casino] takes a cut on each spin of the wheel, paying out less in winnings than it collects in bets. So roulette is a negative-sum game, and so is your non-index mutual fund [actively managed fund]."
>
> **Meir Statman**
> **Journalist**

---

14   Philip Coggan. "The fund-management industry has done very well – but mainly for itself." *The Economist*, Special Report, "Money for Old Hope." 01.03.2008.
See technical note, "The various levels of fees.", page 81

trading. To the banker, the worst client is one who just wants to stay put and refuses to trade his shares. If every client were like that, the manager would earn no more than a simple shopkeeper.

The Kickback

Of all the types of fees, the kickback is the most insidious.

> *Your advisor suggests you acquire some Japanese stocks. He's not a specialist in that market, however, and doesn't know which stocks to buy or sell. He finds a vendor with expertise on Japan to handle this process for him. Let's say he decides to go with a Japanese investment fund. Because the Japanese fund is selling its product through your advisor, it gives him a commission. This type of commission is called a "kickback."*

Therefore, each vendor adds onto its price a kickback for the distributors. This means that most finance managers are actually being paid by vendors when they place their clients' money. Though it may seem unremarkable as a way to make a living, this practice has significant consequences in the choice of investments, encouraging the advisor to consider his own profit first—often to the investor's detriment. If we transpose this situation to the pharmaceutical industry, we would have doctors taking kickbacks from drug makers to prescribe their drugs. Now imagine that those kickbacks were three times as high as the price you paid for your office visit....

Why does an advisor choose one fund over another? Here is where wealth management becomes fraught with conflicts of interest.[15] After all, how can you really tell that your manager has chosen a particular vendor for the quality of its product rather than the size of the cut he gets?[16] While we might be mindful of transaction fees, most of the time

---

15

– Some countries have, in fact, taken measures to address this issue. Beginning in 2012 Independent Financial Advisors in the United Kingdom must charge fees to clients and they will not be able to earn transaction-linked commissions.

– Hilary Osborne. "Financial Advisers' Commission to Cease, Says FSA." *guardian.co.uk*, 26.03.2010.

– Confédération Suisse, Office fédéral des assurances sociales, communiqué sur les rétrocessions, http://www.bsv.admin.ch/aufsichtbv/02024/02064/index.html?lang=fr, 08.04.2010.

16 Pierre Novello, "Le point sur les commissions d'émission et les rétrocessions," *Le Temps*, 03.02.2010.

we're unaware of kickbacks. Kickbacks never appear on our statement. Yet this insidious system has very harmful repercussions.

The Performance Fee

With a fabulous flair for marketing, some managers have devised an alluring formula: namely, the performance fee. They tell the investor that they will charge him less if he doesn't get a certain return on his investments. The flip side is that if the investments do well, the manager takes a bigger percentage than he normally would.

Though it sounds like a win-win proposition, in fact it gives the manager a strong incentive to generate maximum growth—and that is precisely the problem. To reap the rewards of this arrangement, the manager is forced to take high risks with your money. He is encouraged to invest in more speculative stocks. If he succeeds, then everyone's happy. On the other hand, if he proves not so lucky, only you suffer the loss.

Conclusion

Remember the four types of investment fees:

- Fees that are known, understood, and visible (management fee)
- Fees that are known, but their extent is not recognized (transaction fee)
- Invisible fees leading to conflicts of interest (kickback)
- Fees that are known and visible, but their danger is not recognized (performance fee)

As a rule, hidden and indirect fees are at least as great as the management fee that the client is aware of paying and often two to five times greater.

This system has two results: first, your advisor isn't working exclusively in your interest; second, his fees are nibbling away at your wealth.

You may be under the impression that you're paying the bank to defend your interests and grow your money, but in light of these expenses, you might well wonder just who the specialist is working for!

Given the extent of these hidden and indirect fees, the finance industry has no interest in promoting passive management—which, as we shall see, harbors none of these fees.

4.
All Investments Are Based on Prediction

The Mechanisms of Speculation

Every investment recommendation—however serious, precise, and logical it may be—rests on a prediction. It's a wager on the future, uncertain by definition, which makes beating the market an illusory goal. An enormous amount of energy goes into tracking trends, sectors, or securities that seem undervalued in order to bet on their potential and get a better return. The marketing work begins when the banker rationalizes these predictions to mask their random, uncertain nature.

> "Prediction is very difficult, especially if it's about the future."
>
> **Niels Bohr**
> **Nobel Laureate in Physics**

This colossal machine of the finance industry is so creative and sophisticated that it's generated millions of different financial products. But this seemingly infinite diversity really boils down to three kinds of bets:

- **Stock picking**:[17] *The trader decides to buy Shell or Total stocks after studying the characteristics of these companies. The choice is based on the intrinsic value of the shares, given that the companies are*

---

17   See technical note, "Stock picking.", page 83

robust (as revealed by their operating plans, their sales figures, their share of the market, and so on). This method of stock picking can be applied to indexes as well as securities; for instance, in choosing between France (CAC 40) and Germany (DAX), or between Japan and China, etc.

- **Market timing**[18] focuses more on the vitality of the markets at a specific point in time.

> "Beware of financial innovation. Why? Because most of it is designed to enrich the innovators, not investors."
> **John C. Bogle**
> **Founder of Vanguard**

- **Manager selection**[19] consists of counting on a particular specialist, bank, fund, or wealth manager.... This amounts to a wager on his efficiency and tenacity, a bet on his future capacity to grow your money.

Although each product offered on the market seems different and unique, they all derive from one of these three types of speculation. Sprinkled throughout the finance pages of the daily paper and elaborated through the banker's long and convincing list of sales points, these thousands of funds and other financial products always suggest that you can outperform the market.[20]

Beating the Market: Active Management's Holy Grail

Few investors realize that the positions that make up their portfolio are based on prediction—which makes them mere speculation.

Work begins with the analysts, who explore the markets to find the most promising investments. Once they determine that a certain stock might rise faster than others they issue a recommendation to money managers and stockbrokers, who then invest in it. These champions of finance have considerable resources to help them determine

---

18   See technical note, "Market timing." , page 85
19   See technical note, "Manager selection." , page 87
20   "(...) no expert can help you increase your control over the future." Anil Gaba, Robin Hogarth, and Spyros Makridakis. *Dance with Chance*. Oxford: Oneworld Publications, 2009: 11.

whether all the parameters surrounding these investments might lead to unexpected growth. In fact, when the market is free of turbulence, what they have predicted may come to pass. As soon as the value of the stock goes up, word spreads and all the buyers rush in, hoping to reap a profit. Then, by selling at that precise moment, our experts attain their final goal, realizing a return that is above the average for all other transactions. In other words, they have "beaten the market."

> "The road to financial perdition begins with a call to your broker who claims to be able to 'beat the markets' "
>
> **Daniel R. Solin**
> **Author and financial adviser**

It is indeed a spectacular grail, the result of a risky quest that becomes increasingly complicated when our intermediaries (bankers and brokers) step in between supply and demand.

Let's go back to our fish market. In the course of a day, the average price of cod among all the stands goes up to $8/lb.—a price established by calculating the average of all transactions, with some fishermen selling at $5, $6, or $7/lb., while the luckier ones get $9, $10, or $11. Thus, from the time the market opened to the time it closed, the price of fish fluctuated between $5 and $11/lb.

The minute the broker enters into these trades, a certain percentage instantly disappears in transaction fees.

Let's say our broker brings in another trader, a speculator who is neither a fisherman nor a consumer. After having observed the market, this trader begins to buy fish at $11/lb., hoping to resell it at $15. If he succeeds, he will have made a profit of $4 without having produced anything at all.

Our fish broker analyzes the market and gives his prediction to the fisherman: "As of this moment, the price of fish is $11/lb. However, by the end of the day, as the studies of our eminent analysts confirm, it will rise to $15. If I were you, I'd start buying your neighbor's stock."

The broker convinces the fisherman who was selling his fish to become a buyer; a worker becomes a speculator. His risk grows considerably. Regardless of whether he makes a profit or loses money, the broker always profits, because he takes his commissions.

And that is a "fish bone" that is hard to swallow: even if the losses themselves aren't significant. When the banker bets on the "wrong fish," you have to include his commissions in your losses.

> "Why pay people to gamble with your money?"
> **William F. Sharpe**
> **Nobel Laureate in Economics**

Conclusion

Heads or tails?

The coin spins in the air. In this game of chance, the odds of winning are one in two. You've paid a middleman to flip the coin for you, predict the result, and catch that coin before it falls.

Active management is characterized by a frenzy of buying and selling based on predictions. Multiplying transactions, and thereby fees and commissions, in an effort to do better than the market average, is in fact the traditional method chosen by bankers (and most investors) to grow a portfolio.

> "An economist is an expert who will know tomorrow why the things he predicted yesterday didn't happen today"
> **Laurence J. Peter**
> **Nobel Laureate in Economics**

If you buy fish at $11/lb. in order to resell it at $15 in the hopes of realizing a greater profit than everyone else, it's possible to win but also to lose.

The pleasure of winning generally pales in comparison to the disappointment of losing. Thus a major consequence of traditional money management—active management—is that the investor is bound to be disappointed.[21]

21
– Yves Genier. "L'insatisfaction d'une perte est plus forte que le plaisir d'un gain." *Le Temps*, 29.09.2007.
– See technical note, "Few managers beat the markets." , page 93

This is why an investor

who tries passive management

never looks back.

Part II:
How to Invest with Peace of Mind

There are simple ways to manage your money calmly and avoid disappointments. They are based on a number of principles, the two most important being:

- financial planning
- a passive portfolio that enables you to invest without predictions

---

Google's Millionaires

In summer 2004, Google was preparing to go public—an event that promised to transform completely the lives of the company's high-tech employees. The initial public offering of its shares would turn hundreds into millionaires overnight and dozens into multimillionaires. There would even be a couple of newly created billionaires.

All around the world, private bankers were licking their chops at the thought of these employees becoming their clients.

For his part, Google executive Jonathan Rosenberg started to worry about his colleagues, fearing that these soon-to-be millionaires would fall prey to voracious financial advisors. He organized a lecture series on investments to give them the keys to understanding the finance world so they could make educated choices.

Having heard what some of the most eminent economics professors on the planet had to say—namely, William Sharpe, Burton Malkiel, and John Bogle—the Google geeks were ready to confront the wolves on Wall Street.

Then the "beauty pageant" began. Bankers flew in on private jets from the four corners of the globe to parade their products, with gushing speeches and dazzling incentives. But they were taken aback at the techies' response. The Google employees grilled them on how they were able to beat the market and what fees, commissions, and kickbacks they received. Their main question was "Can you guarantee us at least the market rate of return?"

Disconcerted, the bankers tried to bury that information with fabulous promises: "Are you kidding? We'll do much better than the market! We have access to privileged information. You'll get the best investments. You'll be our number one clients...," and so on and so forth.

Each time, however, the same question returned, calmly canceling their arguments. "Well, then? Can you guarantee us at least the market rate of return?"

Without that guarantee, the Google millionaires knew full well that the game was not worth a candle. Instead, they chose passive investment, so that they could become—and remain—happy millionaires.[22]

---

22   Six years later, in spite of the bankers' persistence, Google employees remain passive and peaceful investors.

1.
Active Management and Passive Management

The system of active portfolio management calls to mind Jean de La Fontaine's hare, in his version of Aesop's fable recounting that animal's race against the tortoise (book 6, fable 10).

> *Each of the two animals has bet that it will win the race. But at the starting block, the hare can't be bothered with the competition; he knows he's faster, and he blithely lets the tortoise take off alone* "He makes himself content to wait / And let the tortoise go her gait / In solemn, senatorial state./ She starts; she moils on, modestly and lowly / And with a prudent wisdom hastens slowly." *Thus, the tortoise gets farther and farther ahead, until finally she nears the finish line. Suddenly seeing this, the hare sprints to catch up. But it's too late: the tortoise has already won!*

The tortoise personifies our passive investor, while the hare is like the active investment manager.

A fabulous runner, Mr. Hare is all too aware of his fine qualities. He might well have beaten the tortoise—if he hadn't been sidetracked by other things, such as letting his pride get in the way. After all, he is a specialist: he knows exactly how the race is run, and he basks in the illusion that he can control every turn.[23] So he spends his time in all sorts of pursuits—other than simply pushing ahead as the tortoise does. He examines other routes that might get him there more quickly, calculates the speed relative to the wind, reads up on the best running shoes, and so on. Ironically, all these efforts to find a faster way only slow him down, and he ends up losing the advantage he had boasted of at the start.

In active investing, the speculator or banker is equally distracted. He has extremely sophisticated research tools—some verging on the preposterous[24]—to help him locate products that outperform the rest. But all these analyses take time and energy—to say nothing of the whole marketing operation that gets launched to persuade the client to follow his predictions: business trips, slick brochures, wining and dining, and so forth.

Bankers work hard to grow their clients' capital, but they often get bogged down in activities that distract them from their goals. As financial experts, they labor under the delusion that they master the markets.

The Hare's Fleeting Triumphs vs. the Tenacity of the Tortoise

Obviously, some active investors will succeed from time to time. Their triumphs, however, are in no way systematic, but are rather based on speculation. Most of these experts are so busy examining all the different races that they're often led astray. Meanwhile, the passive investor never deviates from his path. Like the tortoise, he advances—slowly but surely.

Here one might well ask: Why is the tortoise's victory so certain? In other words, how does the passive investor manage to obtain a better return than the active investor? Several studies have shown that about 30 % of active investors will indeed beat the market over

---

23   D. Kahnemann, E. Higgens, and W. Riepe. "Aspects of Investor Psychology." *Journal of Portfolio Management* 24:4 (1998): 52–65.
24   See technical note, "Types of financial analysis." , page 91

the course of a year.[25] But over a longer period, that percentage dwindles.

Let's say we have a hundred people in a casino and can track their daily results. The first day, thirty people win while seventy leave with less money than they had when they arrived. The next day, the same hundred gamblers return to try their luck. At the end of the day, we again have thirty winners and seventy losers— but they're not all the same people in each group as before. The story repeats itself day after day. When the casino closes, there's always a similar proportion of losers and winners, but they're never all the same. A fellow who was down on his luck one day can be a winner the next, but he's still behind in his winnings, and there's no assurance that he'll hit the jackpot the following day. Conversely, someone who's had a lucky streak all week long can suddenly lose all his winnings and never manage to catch up again.

> "It's just not true that you can't beat the market. Every year about one-third of the fund managers do it. Of course, each year it is a different group."
> **Robert Stovall**
> **Asset Manager**

The tortoise is under pressure, too. She struggles to advance into the wind (a market downturn, falling stock prices); she picks up her pace under better conditions (a market upswing). But no matter what happens, she forges ahead.[26]

Passive management eliminates all speculative decisions in order to capture only the markets' powerful performance.[27]

---

25   See technical note, "Few managers beat the markets." , page 93

26

– Prof. L. Barras, O. Scaillet, and R. Wermers. Swiss Finance Institute. "False Discoveries in Mutual Fund Performance: Measuring Luck in Estimated Alphas," Research Paper Series N°08-18, 2008.
– Andy Baker, *The Economist*, Special Report "Money for old hope." 01.03.2008.
– Alfred Cowles III. "Can Stock Market Forecasters Forecast?" *Econometria* 1:3 (1933): 309–324.
– "DALBAR Study Shows Market Timers Lose Their Money," press release, April 2004.
– James L. Davis. "Mutual Fund Performance and Manager Style," *Financial Analyst Journal* 57:1 (2001): 19–27.
– Eugene F. Fama and Kenneth R. French. "Luck versus Skill in the Cross Section of Mutual Fund Returns," *Journal of Finance* (December 2009).
– Michael Jensen. "The Performance of Mutual Funds in the Period 1945–1964," *Journal of Finance* 23:2 (1967): 389–416.
– Pat Regnier. "Can You Outsmart the Market?" *Fortune Magazine*, 21.12.2009.
– Jason Zweig. "Why Many Investors Keep Fooling Themselves," *Wall Street Journal*, 16.01.2010.

27   Contrary to what one might imagine, this strategy wins, even in the short term.

Awareness of Risk Brings Peace of Mind

There is nothing "passive" about the passive investor. He has simply understood that he can neither predict nor control the market. Because of this, he actively focuses on the things he is able to influence.[28]

To avoid getting caught up in the enormous pressures of the market the passive investor chooses to accept them, which gives him a calmer outlook on his investments. He takes a disciplined approach based on solid rules to strike a balance between what the market has to offer and the level of risk he can tolerate.

Now, which animal do you think would stay calmer over the course of this long race: the tortoise or the hare? The hare—the active investor—who runs on adrenaline, bouncing from delirious joy to cruel disillusion? Or the tortoise—the passive investor—who never pushes beyond her limits but steadily pursues her goal at her own pace?

Of course, not everyone is the same when it comes to stress. For some hares this frenzied race is an endless source of delight. They're the impetuous types, with an adventurous spirit and an exhilarating penchant for risk. Gambling is their lifeblood and the stock market their casino.

It is certainly not as sexy to be a tortoise—to "hasten slowly." Even though this method is more effective, it seems to pale in comparison.

If the adrenaline rush thrills you, and you're able to keep your distance (in terms of stress) from the frenetic transactions of active management—and if, above all, you fully accept the risks—then there is no need for you to change your financial ways.

When an investor like the tortoise tries on the hare's running shoes, however, he must understand that he may lose his shell. It's crucial to understand the risks of active speculation for your portfolio; after all, not everyone is willing to play roulette with a pension fund or a retire-

---

28
- Tim Hale. *Smarter Investing: Simpler Decisions for Better Results*, 2nd ed. Harlow, U.K.: Pearson Education Ltd, 2009:85.
- Ellen Langer. "The Illusion of Control." *Journal of Personality and Social Psychology* 32:2 (1975): 311-328.

ment egg nest.[29] If you can't afford to lose your capital, then it's wiser to behave like the tortoise.

Having read this far, you may find that the tortoise profile speaks to you more than that of the hare. Now that we know how the hare operates, let's look at what it takes to become a tortoise.

ACTIVE Speculation

---

29   See technical note, "'Core' and 'satellite' portfolios." , page 99

2.
Your Copilot and Your Road Map

In the hare's mind, investing is a competitive sport, a race against the clock to score record returns. His opponents are the market and the other speculators.

The tortoise, however, isn't looking to win a medal, knowing that she could well lose everything in the attempt. Instead, her foremost aim is to maintain her financial well-being.

"What if your advisor talks only about returns, not risk? ...It's his job to take risk into account by telling you the range of possible outcomes you face. If he won't, go to a new planner, someone who will get real."

William F. Sharpe
Nobel Laureate in Economics

There are those who run the marathon because they want to get there first, no matter what it takes—even if it means risking the money they started out with. Others pursue a reasonable goal, tailored to their means and their physical capacity, for the sake of preserving their capital.

Instead of dreaming of miraculous gains while turning a blind eye to the danger, the tortoise seeks to reach her goal calmly and deliberately. Her concept of the race emphasizes her own well-being rather than the challenge of competition.

Still, like any athlete, the passive investor needs to prepare for the marathon. He does this by working out with a good trainer.

Steering your portfolio onto a passive course, though simple in theory, is complex in practice. That is why it is important to have a "coach"—an investment counselor.[30]

A Copilot for Your Portfolio

Unlike a banker, the partner you're looking for should not be a seller who receives a commission. He needs to be a "copilot" who will help you find the best route to reach your own finish line. He lays out the road map, planting the mileposts and establishing the necessary reference points to let you know where you are with your investments.[31]

Passive management begins with careful planning. From that point on, you have a single, clear-cut course to follow. Convoluted explanations are not needed—and neither are all the costs that come with them. Your copilot simply makes sure you stick to your plan.

The Copilot's Compensation

How should your manager or copilot be paid? His advisory fee should be fair: a balanced price that gives the manager the means to do his work while also assuring the client the most objective and transparent service.[32]

30
– There are several kinds of copilots, to suit various needs and budgets. See technical note, "Tips on choosing a good copilot." , page 101
– Richard Ferri. *The power of passive investing*, http://video.forbes.com/fvn/personalfinance/richard-ferri-power-of-passive-investing?partner=contextual

31   D. Kahnemann, E. Higgens, and W. Riepe. "Aspects of Investor Psychology." *Journal of Portfolio Management* 24:4 (1998): 52–65.

32   Whether you pay a fixed amount or a percentage depends on the type of copilot (see technical note, "Tips on choosing a good copilot", page 101). The important thing is to make sure that all the money he receives comes from you, not from any commissions paid by a third party for his work.

*Passive managers must be paid exclusively by the inves-
tor, receiving no form of commission or kickback. Nor may they
collect fees based on performance.[33] Regardless of the client's
profile—whether he seeks a more conservative portfolio or a riskier
one—the manager is paid the same fee.*

This means that finally you have concrete knowledge of how your manager earns his money[34]: you can figure out his motives and understand
his actions. Free of any obligation to get results for a bank or for his
own benefit, he devotes his competence to properly managing your
portfolio. Gone are the speculations and distractions that separated
the manager's goals from those of the investor. Purged of conflicts of
interest, the relationship of trust with the "financial copilot" becomes
legitimate and justified. Directed by his advice, you radically minimize
your fees and obtain market performance, which is your due.

Pitfalls to Avoid in Choosing a Copilot

A tortoise would not choose a hare as her trainer if she wanted effective support. Likewise, a passive investment plan cannot be carried out
by a traditional active manager, particularly one who works for a bank.

What's more, it's important to watch out for hares disguised as tortoises. **Passive management—which has proven effective for almost
forty years in institutional settings[35]—has begun to inspire imitators.**
More and more wealth managers specialize in and provide passive financial products. That would be good news for investors—except that
the way most of these new managers use the products still involves
some speculation.[36] This runs counter not only to the nature of passive
management, but also to the very thing that guarantees its effectiveness: the fact that it eliminates all prediction.

33
– Mark Grinblatt and Sheridan Titman. "The Impact of Performance-based Fees on Pension Fund
   Management." Finance Working Paper, Anderson Graduate School of Management, University of
   California at Los Angeles, rev. February 1987.
– Ian Cowie. "Warren Buffett 'Fund' Illustrates Rip off Management Charges." *Daily Telegraph*,
   29.09.2010.
34   See technical note, "The various levels of fees." , page 81
35   Richard A. Ferri. *All about Index Funds.* New York: McGraw-Hill, 2002: 36–41.
36   See the section, "Hares disguised as tortoises," chapter 5, page 69

To determine whether a manager truly provides passive management, ask him how he is compensated. This straightforward question will give you a good idea of his motivations. Next, ask him how he intends to meet your goals. This will help you confirm that his approach does not entail any kind of prediction.[37]

Setting Your Goals and Creating a Financial Plan[38]

Together with your copilot, you need to find out where your own finish line is located. Why are you entering the race? What are your dreams? What are your fears? What are your expectations for now and for the future? Your copilot will help you set this goal, much as a nutritionist identifies the ideal weight when planning a weight-loss program. The passive manager will determine whether your means suffice to meet your goal, and if they don't, he will guide you to a more realistic goal.

The tortoise, once she has formulated her objective (making sure she can live comfortably, have a good retirement, buy a house, and so on), examines the various routes to find the one best suited to her goals.[39] "I'd like to arrive at this milepost by such and such a time." Which road should she take? And how far should she go each day?

Your advisor has the compass and gauge and all the tools of the trade. Together you can establish an ideal financial plan and a clear and comprehensible program. Once the itinerary has been mapped out, it has an immediate psychological impact. This process prevents you from reacting emotionally to the fluctuations in your investments, because you know you have a direction you must follow. You know where you're going now, at what pace, and by what means. Above all, you have the assurance that by sticking to your course, you will arrive at your destination.

37   See technical note. "Tips on choosing a good copilot." , page 101
38   See technical note, "Setting your goals and creating a financial plan." , page 103
39   David Bogoslaw."Retirement: Goal-based Investing Gains Traction." *Bloomberg Businessweek*, 18.08.2009.

The New Role of the Bank

What becomes of the banker in this new setup? Although most of the financial products sold by the bank are no longer useful to you, you still need certain services, such as transfers, deposit of securities, accounting, and credit cards. So from now on you use the institution only as a "safe" to hold your assets. You won't let the banker choose how to invest your money anymore—those decisions are yours alone, and can't be influenced by an outsider with his own interests in the mix.

3.
The Recipe for the Best Portfolio

Illusions and Reality

Finance has a dangerous side: the dazzling dream of sensational gains. It's important never to let yourself get caught up in that dream.

After all, would you be tempted by a weight-loss pill that was supposed to make you lose 25 lbs. without dieting? You can just imagine yourself on the beach, happily soaking up the sun in your new bathing suit. That's the same lure of fantasy that every investor must learn to filter out, because it completely blinds them to the risks. They don't consider the side effects or health dangers; all they can think of is the miracle promised by the deceptive drug: A record return! A golden opportunity!

Such fantasies only prevent us from exercising sound critical judgment.

> "Building a portfolio around index fund...is just refusing to believe in magic."
>
> **Bethany McLean**
> **Editor Fortune Magazine**

U nlike active management, the passive philosophy is based on actual facts. Its method and effectiveness derive from scientific observation of the markets. It's a commonsense approach that has been irrefutably proven.[40]

In preparing for any race, you first assess the environment, the terrain, and the other runners in order to uncover advantages and disadvantages, strengths and weaknesses, and to avoid potential problems. Thus, our tortoise has studied the route, observing all the road signs— the concrete data on which to

> "Those who have knowledge, don't predict. Those who predict, don't have knowledge."
>
> **Lao Tzu**
> **Chinese philosopher**

base her investments—as well as all the obstacles—those failures she needs to circumvent. This allows her to figure out the best course and the most suitable investments. What solid and reliable information can she glean from examining the markets?

The Ingredients of a Traditional Portfolio

To establish the right asset allocation, the manager first determines the client's investment profile. The client needs to decide whether he is more "conservative"—favoring safe investments—or more "aggressive"—emphasizing maximum growth. In order to situate their clients between these two extremes, banks have come up with an infinite array of profiles (defensive, neutral, balanced, moderate, dynamic), each of them corresponding to a proportionate mix of fixed income (such as bonds, which offer relative security) and risky assets (such as stocks, which provide relative growth).

All financial products can be divided between these two categories.[41] A portfolio with a "balanced" profile might consist of 50% stocks and 50% bonds, while an "aggressive" profile might mean 90% stocks (in hopes of obtaining maximum growth) and 10% bonds.

---

40   See technical note, "From academic research to passive management." , page 107
41   In passive management, all investments fall into two main categories: stocks and bonds.
– See technical note, "Stocks and bonds." , page 111
– See technical note, "Dividing a portfolio among financial instruments." , page 113

An active manager generally adheres to the profile assigned and the proportion of security vs. growth chosen, but then chooses securities very different in nature from a variety of sectors. The endless combinations generate extremely complex financial setups.

The features of any single product give rise to a series of bets. To purchase a simple bond, for example, the active manager must choose when (first bet), the country (second bet), the sector of activity (third bet), the company within that sector (fourth bet), and the length of the loan (fifth bet), either long term (up to thirty years) or short term (between six and twelve months).

A traditional portfolio isn't solely made up of these sorts of products, however; it includes many far more sophisticated ones as well. So if a simple bond can entail up to five different choices, how many more bets would these more complex products involve? Ten? Twenty? One hundred? Given that a traditional portfolio contains several dozen products, the number of bets further multiplies—not just in the choice of each individual product but also the overall combination of products. And that is just for one client's portfolio....

Passive management eliminates all this complexity.

Risks and Returns Are Related

>   *It's more prudent to admire parachute jumps with your feet on solid ground than to experience them in the sky. Without the danger of free fall, however, you'll never taste that unique sensation of floating through the clouds.*

Taking risks can lead to greater gains than the absence of risk: everyday life suggests this, and the markets prove it.

A conservative investment profile is more prudent but far less gratifying in terms of profits. The less you risk, the less you stand to gain; conversely, increasing your risk enables you to draw a better yield. Risks and returns are inevitably related.[42]

42
− William F. Sharpe. "Capital Asset Prices: A Theory of Market Equilibrium under Conditions of Risk." *Journal of Finance* 19:3 (1964): 425–442.
− Jeremy J. Siegel, *Stocks for the Long Run.* New York: McGraw-Hill, 1998.

Before the race, the tortoise and her copilot examined the hare's "equipment." Does a traditional portfolio contain any component that might come close to zero risk?

Stocks, which are risky assets, are immediately out of the picture. Fixed revenues, however, can also prove uncertain. Even low-risk corporate bonds, for instance, depend on the health of the company. Finance history has witnessed the failure of even the most solid and prestigious corporations.

> "Some investments do have higher expected returns than others. Which ones? Well, by and large they're the ones that will do the worst in bad times."
>
> **William F. Sharpe**
> **Nobel Laureate in Economics**

The same goes for banks; just think of Lehman Brothers. Contrary to what people usually think, the cash you deposit in your bank account is also an investment, because if the bank fails, you lose everything.[43]

What else can we do? Buy a house? That might be a safe investment, but suppose you later need cash equal to a quarter of its value: you have to sell the whole property to get it. So would it be better just to keep your cash under a mattress? Or buy gold and lock it in a safe? All these solutions likewise pose risks (storage, protection, insurance, etc.).

Government Bonds: The Least Risky Assets

Researching safe investments, the tortoise is intrigued by government bonds.[44]

– Sidney Homer., *A History of Interest Rates*. New Brunswick, NJ: Rutgers University Press, 1963.

– Eugene F. Fama and Kenneth R. French. "The Cross-Section of Expected Stock Returns." *Journal of Finance* 47 (1992): 427–465.

– Eugene F. Fama and Kenneth R. French. "Value versus Growth: The International Evidence." *Journal of Finance* 53 (December 1998)

– Ombudsman des banques suisses. "Rendement élevé égal risque élevé." http://www.bankingombudsman.ch, communiqué of 07.07.2009.

43   See technical note, "Why it's risky to hold cash." , page 115

44   See technical note, "Why government bonds are the safest investment." , page 117

Here's a little scenario:

Let's say you have $100 to invest.

If you lend it to the government at an interest rate of 1%, by the end of the year you'll have $101—no matter what happens. Because this borrower can simply print the money it needs to pay you back.

If you lend your $100 to Coca-Cola or Sony, they promise you more (2%, or $102 for the same term). But even though this transaction seems more profitable, doubling your return, if the company defaults—an uncontrollable risk—you stand to lose everything, both the interest and your capital.

So which do you prefer? The guaranteed $101 in government bonds? Or the risky $102 in corporate bonds?

There are those who will argue that a business like Coca-Cola isn't about to go belly-up. Stop and think about it: have we ever seen a giant market player collapse? Yes or no? Should it happen, you'll go from $100 capital to $0. Nada. Do you have the means to shoulder that risk? And is it really worth it?

On the one hand, you earn a meager return that guarantees your capital. On the other, you earn twice the interest, but with no guarantee that you will get even your initial investment back. As the saying goes, you can't have it both ways.

That is why short-term government bonds in your own currency[45] are incontestably the least risky security on the market (which doesn't mean they're infallible, as the recent events in Greece and Ireland or Spain and Portugal have shown).

Here's another brief exercise that may help in discussions with your financial advisor. Short-term (one year) government bonds, being the least risky investment, have a very low yield (let's say it's 1%). So what should you make of a so-called "no-risk" investment that would give you 4%? You know there's always a risk somewhere, but where? Thus your question would

---

45   See technical note, "Short-term government bonds in your country's currency." , page 119.

be: who guarantees this 4%, and how? And why is it that this investment pays four times more than government bonds?

Companies Create Value

Our tortoise has finally found a solid investment that guarantees she won't lose her initial capital, which is all she has—her shell. Because risk and return are related, however, she knows that short-term government bonds will give her only a meager return.[46]

Invested solely in government bonds, the tortoise can guarantee her security. She can reach the finish line with her house intact on her back—but she will get there very slowly. What can she do if she wants to increase her speed—that is, the return on her portfolio? Together with her advisor, she goes over the map again and studies the possible routes.

The products the banker proposed? Certainly not! I want to invest in something I understand, whose risks I can assess. As for real estate,[47] hunting down and purchasing property is a long and tedious process, to say nothing of management and upkeep and whatever problems might arise. The same goes for any kind of business, a restaurant or a shop that could easily go under. Gambling at the casino? Buying lottery tickets? Those aren't "good" risks either. The odds of winning are slim, while those of losing are huge.

Such a quandary requires you to think critically, as the tortoise is doing here. If an opportunity arises as you explore your options, don't hesitate to take it. As long as you fully understand the nature of the investment, acknowledge its limitations, and evaluate its risks lucidly and

> "Investors...can't pick stocks that are better than average. Stocks are a good thing to own over time. There's only two things you can do wrong: You can buy the wrong ones, and you can buy or sell them at the wrong time."
>
> **Warren Buffett**
> **Chairman of Berkshire Hathaway**

---

46   See technical note, "Government bonds and inflation." , page 121

47   Real estate is an excellent investment, as long as you own the house or building directly. Don't buy real estate through an investment fund or a financial vehicle, as these only increase volatility and fees. Direct property ownership protects you against local inflation and generally gives you a good return.

objectively, there is no need to wait: just go for it! No banker, no financial strategy, no book on finance (not even this one!) should influence your decision at that point. Good sense is worth every bit as much as the advice of the best specialists.

For her part, the tortoise continued her research in hopes of identifying "the" investment that, combined with bonds, might put her ahead. Thus, she interviewed all the previous winners to find out what they did to win. Likewise, you should take a look around you: who has made money and how? You probably don't need more than one hand to count the hares—those speculators or lottery winners who have struck it rich. So speculation and lottery tickets aren't the path you want to take. Keep looking. After you have identified everyone who has done well, ask yourself what they have in common. Could it be that at one time or another, they all profited from the growth of their companies? Some companies grow considerably and become Nestlé or Microsoft, while others fail for any number of reasons. Overall, however, the fabric of the economy grows.

Thus, in spite of bankruptcies and crises, corporations are one investment category that, on average, creates value.[48] And that potential gain is not about one specific company in one specific sector; it's about the corporation as an economic entity within the system as a whole.

That entity begins with an idea that is made concrete through work, which itself is financed through the infusion of capital. None of these three elements creates value on its own: if there is no sound idea to start with, there is no point having money to invest in a workforce. Likewise, without capital, there won't be a workforce to realize a sound idea—and so on.

If each of the three, however, makes good use of the other two, the risks pay off. The union of these three factors produces value and generates new capital. This in turn profits all three—the idea, the work, and the capital all earn money—as well as the system as a whole, because they help it progress toward greater growth.[49]

---

48   See technical note, "Creating value: stocks." , page 123
49   Adam Smith. An Inquiry into the Nature and Causes of the Wealth of Nations, 1776.

An unbeatable return!

An investor who placed his $ 100,000 in the S&P 500 in 1940 would today have $ 131,000,000—that's right: 131 million![50] And that's without trying to use any "market timing"[51] or "stock picking,"[52] and without flinching at the defaults and crises that took place over all those years. The process of creating value, as companies do, simply works. It's more powerful than any fund manager could ever be.[53]

Maximum Diversification

Investing in a company is a risk that earns a fair reward. But to get it, you have to invest in the right stocks—it's the old issue of speculation again! Because our tortoise can't read a crystal ball, she thought hard about how to get around that problem. Individual companies may shrink or grow, but on the whole companies progress. So to avoid speculation, why not invest in all the companies on the planet? That would be the most logical solution.

When you invest in all companies, through passive funds or index funds, you know for certain that it's impossible to lose everything.[54] Some companies will take off, while others will go under. Passive management understands this law and doesn't see it as a problem. Instead, it takes advantage of the fact that there is no point trying to choose and no need to make predictions.[55]

50　　According to S&P Index Services Group.

51　　See technical note, "Market timing." , page 85

52　　See technical note, "Stock picking." , page 83

53　　This same phenomenon occurs in all national markets. For example,

–　If his Swiss aunt placed CHF 100,000 among every Swiss stock on the market in 1940, she'd have CHF 35,000,000 today (Pictet & Cie. The Performance of Shares and Bonds in Switzerland, update, January 2010).

–　If his British cousin had invested £100,000 in the FTSE sixteen years later (in 1956, when the FTSE was created), today he'd have £47,000,000 (according to the FTSE UK).

54　　Of course, all the stocks on the planet could fall, but by how much?

55

–　Share prices are unpredictable: Paul A. Samuelson. "Proof That Properly Anticipated Prices Fluctuate Randomly." *Industrial Management Review* 6:2 (1965): 41.

–　As John Bogle writes in *Common Sense on Mutual Funds*. Hoboken, NJ: John Wiley & Sons, Inc., 2010: 299: "The chances that individual fund investors will find the holy grail that will identify in advance the future's superior performers seem dismal."

Everyone knows that you reduce your risk considerably by not "putting all your eggs in one basket."[56] And if you take this principle further by investing in all stocks, your portfolio is completely diversified, assuring both performance[57] and security.

Fees Nibble Away at Your Portfolio's Performance

In active investment, the managers' fees make a sizeable dent in the performance of the portfolios they manage. It's simply common sense: the more transactions they make, the more fees they take, and the less you get back in the end. Even knowing all this, it's hard to fully grasp the importance without running the numbers.

As crazy as it may sound, management fees that seem minute (What's 2.5% a year on a million dollars of capital?) nonetheless end up having a dramatic impact on your portfolio over the long term. In fact, in twenty years, that 2.5% paid in fees will represent half of your capital.

It's as if you were to make a massive "donation" of money that is actually due to you! There are plenty of mathematical proofs and graphs showing the unbelievable effect these percentage fees have on performance.

Be sure to read the technical note[58] that shows how, with $1 million of capital, you can give a $2 million donation. The question is, who would you like to donate this money to?

Stop Bleeding Money

One thing is certain: finance companies will keep finding more and more creative ways to claim more and more fees...and to bury them in endless speeches. It's therefore crucial that you do everything possible to reduce these fees that, little by little, gnaw away at your performance. To that end, the choice of a manager who is exclusively paid

---

56   Harry M. Markowitz. Portfolio Selection: Efficient Diversification of Investments. New York: John Wiley & Sons, Inc., 1959.

57   David Booth and Eugene F. Fama. "Diversification Returns and Asset Contributions." *Financial Analysts Journal* (May/June 1992).

58   See technical note, "The impact of compound interest on fees and performance.", page 125

advisory fees, and not commission, will best guarantee that you will diminish your fees and preserve your performance.

A Passive Portfolio

A passive portfolio is made up exclusively of high-quality bonds and world-class stocks, in a proportion predetermined with your copilot according to your goals and your profile.[59]

To this day, it's the **most effective portfolio in balancing risk and return.** It's the only way to invest without speculation, relying solely on facts. Instead of struggling against the market in a vain effort to beat it, **passive management lets the market work for the investor.**

The principles of a successful investor[60]

- Have a financial plan

- Keep in mind that return is proportionate to risk

- Understand your investments

- Profit from the creation of value by companies

- Diminish your risk by diversifying

- Minimize your fees

- Stay the course

---

59   See technical note, "The effect of asset allocation on portfolio performance." , page 129
60   These are merely the basic principles of passive management. There are fifty or so further rules enabling you to increase your return, diminish your risks, and above all avoid pitfalls.

4.
Wealth and Well-Being

Passive management is like the culinary arts. So that we may savor our meal—calmly awaiting the goals of our investments—we have composed a menu (an investment plan) and selected the best products (all the world's stocks and quality bonds). As with any recipe, however, it's not just the ingredients that matter. You still have to know how to prepare them in order to bring out their fullest flavor (security and profit).

How do we "prepare" high-grade bonds and diversified stocks in a passive portfolio? And what are the immediate results of this passive "gastronomy"?

Eliminate Unnecessary Risks

With passive investment, unnecessary risks—those dangers lurking in a traditional portfolio that demand constant vigilance—are eliminated:

- the risk of fraud (being swindled by a Bernie Madoff, for example)
- the risk of trustee bankruptcy (undergone by Lehman Brothers' clients)
- management risk (a manager's bad decisions)
- exchange rate risk
- interest rate risk
- liquidity problems or risk
- company bankruptcy risk[61]

---

61   See technical note, "Unnecessary risks." , page 131

Thanks to your plan of action—one that is solid, reliable, and comprehensible—you have just accomplished the feat of taking charge of your investments. Only a handful of investors before you—representing not even 1% of the world's private wealth—have managed to banish unnecessary risks from their portfolios. It was no easy task; they had to call into question the very tenets of traditional investment. It took courage to reconsider active management, but the results are tangible. You have purged your portfolio of speculation, management fees, and unnecessary risks.

Exploit Unavoidable Risks

Now let's look at the two risks from which you aren't protected: inflation and market volatility. While active management pretends it can fight these risks, the passive investor knows better and instead takes the opportunity to manage them.[62]

In passive management, you know in advance what your maximum risk level is. This knowledge empowers you to make decisions about risk.

Let's say you have a million dollars to invest on behalf of an educational foundation. To ensure that the institution will continue to flourish and offer the best education possible, you want to preserve the capital and have sufficient growth to offset inflation. How should you invest that money?

In passive management, a low-risk position would perhaps divide the portfolio between 20% of all the world's stocks (so, $200,000) and 80% high-grade bonds ($800,000).

Now, let's imagine a worst-case scenario: there's a world economic crisis, and the price of your stocks falls 50%. What would that do to your portfolio? The bonds calmly continue to rise, while the global stocks lose half their value, going from $200,000 to $100,000 in your portfolio. Your maximum loss is

---

62   See technical note, "Inflation and volatility." , page 133

thus 10% of your overall investment—a lesser evil compared to active managers' losses!

Suppose the foundation's directors don't consider a possible 10% loss to be overly great, and they deem a higher level of risk acceptable. You'd then want to increase the proportion of diversified stocks in your portfolio, going to 30% stocks and 70% bonds, or 40% stock and 60% bonds, and so on.

Once the risk of loss has been accepted—or fully "digested"—stress no longer sways the investor. Especially when that investor understands that in the long term, the markets always rise.[63]

Performance

A passive portfolio assures you of an annual performance that adds to your capital.[64] Of course, there is no shortage of hares trying to break the speed record, but the tortoise has time on her side.[65] Day after day, year after year, seven out of ten hares remain on the sidelines.[66] Because at one time or another they will break a foot, lose their way, or fail to hear the starting pistol....

The longer they invest, the farther they fall behind.

---

63   See technical note, "Creating value: stocks." , page 123
64   See technical note, "Passive management: 5% extra performance." , page 135
65
– Prof. L. Barras, O. Scaillet, and R. Wermers. Swiss Finance Institute. "False Discoveries in Mutual Fund Performance: Measuring Luck in Estimated Alphas." *Research Paper Series* N°08-18, 2008.
– Andy Baker. *The Economist*, Special Report, "Money for Old Hope." 01.03.2008.
– Alfred Cowles, III. "Can Stock Market Forecasters Forecast?" *Econometria* 1:3 (1933): 309–324
– DALBAR, Study Shows Market Timers Lose Their Money, press release, April 2004.
– James L. Davis, "Mutual Fund Performance and Manager Style." *Financial Analyst Journal* 57:1 (2001): 19–27.
– Eugene F. Fama and Kenneth R. French, "Luck versus Skill in the Cross Section of Mutual Fund Returns." *Journal of Finance*, December 2009.
– Michael Jensen, "The Performance of Mutual Funds in the Period 1945–1964." *Journal of Finance* 23:2 (1967): 389–416.
– Pat Regnier. "Can You Outsmart the Market?" *Fortune Magazine*, 21.12.2009.
– Jason Zweig, "Why Many Investors Keep Fooling Themselves." *Wall Street Journal*, 16.01.2010.
66   See technical note, "Few managers beat the markets." , page 93

The Illusion of Performance in Active Management

People get so enthralled with winners that they tend to forget the hordes who have lost. A million hares are running the race, but all we see is the one who is on TV. It's just like the lottery: we only read the winner's name in the newspaper, not the endless lists of the unlucky. For each new millionaire, how many have lost everything they put down?

It's just as easy to ignore the risks the winners took. When a manager boasts, "I made 20% last year!" people get ecstatic and start spinning fantasies. No one ever says, "That's fabulous! But if you'd been wrong, how much would you have lost?"

Yet that is the most important question. If he put 10% on the line, then yes, it was brilliant; but if he risked all his capital, the result can't be considered the same way. Thanks to this amnesia, these illusions of "easy" victory, active management gets us to believe we can beat the market and continues to cash in on our dreams.

> "If there's 10,000 people looking at the stocks and trying to pick winners, one in 10,000 is going to score, by chance alone"
>
> **Merton Miller**
> **Nobel Laureate in Economics**

When you're among the 70% who lose money, how do you catch up again? Do you head back to the casino with more money? Wait, you have less than you did to begin with—so what can you do now? Try doubling your risk to recover from your first loss? Perhaps borrow money or take out a mortgage? This is how, blinded by tales of singular performance, people get caught up in thoughtless risks.

Some sprinters will object, "Sure, it's great that you can get ahead in the long term, little tortoise…but in the short term, your pace leaves much to be desired."

However, what better result is there than the assurance that, on any given day, you'll come out ahead of 70% who are in the race?

"Properly measured, the average actively managed dollar must underperform the average passively managed dollar, net of costs. Empirical analyses that appear to refute this principle are guilty of improper measurement."

William F. Sharpe
Nobel Laureate in Economics

5.
The Siren Song

Self-discipline is an essential aspect of passive management.[67] To avoid falling back into the vicious circle of speculation, you need to rely on your experience, your road map, your advisor—and on your best ally: your critical judgment.

There are three main traps to avoid: emotional decisions, hares disguised as tortoises, and the alluring promises of active management.

Emotional Decisions and Crisis Situations

Paradoxically, the person the investor needs to watch out for the most is himself! It takes a certain amount of willpower to ignore all the rumors, the "hot tips," the temptations of "stock picking."[68] "Airbus is adding a new plane to its fleet; it's sure to be a gold mine!" or "Greece is going bankrupt; you'd better sell everything!" and on and on. At such times, the passive investor has to stand firm and resist all the calls to speculation."[69]

"Relax, dear tortoise," your copilot reassures you before the race. "You know how skittish the hare is. Your compass isn't broken; it still points North to your goals.... Just ignore those champion hares, all got up in the latest gear, with their treacherous shortcuts. Sure, everyone's talking about their mind-boggling performance on the training field, but then they run straight down a dead end. You know that."

67   Larry E. Swedroe. *The Only Guide to a Winning Investment Strategy You'll Ever Need*. New York: Truman Talley Books/Dutton, 1998: 219.
68   See technical note, "Stock picking." , page 83
69   See technical note, "Emotional finance." , page 139

Just think of Dominique Strauss Kahn, former managing director of the International Monetary Fund, ranked the seventh most influential leader in the world by Time Magazine.

> "The investor's chief problem - and even his worst enemy—is likely to be himself."
>
> **Benjamin Graham**
> **Legendary investor**
> **Mentor to Warren Buffett**

Because the IMF is a nonprofit public organization, its opinions and forecasts are unbiased by financial or commercial interests. DSK (as he's known) thus became a prime spokesperson for the world of finance, receiving objective analysis and access to resources from the world's greatest economists and benefiting from the best network of information there is. He could, for example, speak directly to Obama, the European Central Bank, or China.

What did the best-placed economist on earth announce to us in the summer of 2008? "The crisis is behind us."[70] But then, during the following six months, the market tumbled. At the end of the year, DSK announced, "The worst is yet to come"—a declaration soon followed by one of the strongest rebounds the market had ever known![71]

If recommendations from someone of that caliber can't be trusted, there is no point wasting time with other winning formulas. The predictions of a well-respected manager—even one of the big names, whose bonuses come to millions a year—are still no more than predictions, plain and simple.

> "Fear has a far greater grasp on human action than does the impressive weight of historical evidence."
>
> **Jeremy Siegel**
> **Professor and economist**

70   FMI, "Strauss-Kahn: la crise financière est 'derrière nous' " www.nouvelobs.com, 23.06.2008, http://tempsreel.nouvelobs.com/actualites/economie/finance_et_marches/20080515.OBS4027/strausskahn__la_crise_financiere_est_derriere_nous.html
71   AFP, "La crise va empirer selon DSK "Le Figaro, 12.12.2008, http://www.lefigaro.fr/flash-actu/2008/12/12/01011-20081212FILWWW00230-la-crise-va-empirer-selon-dsk.php

Self-control is far more challenging when markets plunge in times of crisis.[72] In active management, managers and investors go into panic mode: what should we do? Sell? Buy? To deal with the crisis they place new bets and their stress levels rise in proportion to the risks.

In passive management, however, there is no decision to make, no need for an urgent appointment with your manager. Your meetings have nothing to do with the latest market developments. You understand how risky emotional decisions are, and you're not going to switch position thoughtlessly. You have chosen a certain level of risk on which to base your plan of action—a risk you're fully aware of as you carry out that plan.

> "In the stock market (as in much of life), the beginning of wisdom is admitting your ignorance. One of the many things you cannot know about stocks is exactly when they will go up or go down. Over the long term, stocks generally rise at a nice pace. History shows they double in value every seven years or so. But in the short term, stocks are just plain wild. Over periods of days, weeks and months, no one has any idea what they will do. Still, nearly all investors think they are smart enough to divine such short-term movements. This hubris frequently gets them into trouble."[73]

So whatever situation may arise, have confidence in your chosen route: it's a rational plan based exclusively on facts. By taking back control of your investments, you have already succeeded where the specialists have failed. It's crucial, then, to keep this frame of mind and refuse to be lured by the siren song.

Hares Disguised as Tortoises

Watch out for another type of "music" as well: those counterfeit formulas that try to pass for passive management. As we discussed earlier,[74] some hares disguise themselves as tortoises. These are the managers

---

72 Larry Swedroe. "Lesson from the Bear Market." CBS Moneywatch.com, 09.11.2009. http://money-watch.bnet.com/investing/blog/wise-investing/lessons-from-the-bear-market/974
73 James K. Glassman. "Attempts to Time the Market Always Leave the Investor Out of Sync." New York Times. 12.11.2001.
74 See the section, "Pitfalls to avoid in choosing a copilot." in part II, chapter 2, page 47.

who call themselves "passive" while their reflexes are still speculative. They employ the mechanisms and tools of passive management and are more conscious about managing risk, but their investment decisions remain influenced by predictive analysis. Various techniques represent this approach.

Halfway between active and passive management, for example, is index management, which consists of buying index funds rather than corporate stock (or S&P instead of Nestlé). This formula is safer because it avoids "stock picking,"[75] which means less betting is involved, It's still based on predictive selection, however, choosing one country over another—lots of China, not too much Japan, and so on. It's like playing a modified version of roulette that eliminates the even vs. odd bets but keeps the red vs. black bets, thus retaining half the risk.[76]

"Market timing"[77] is equally dangerous. Here, managers analyze the health of the markets and bet on the best moment to get in or out, ostensibly for the sake of prudence. At the casino, "market timing" would be like never playing on a certain day of the week, because supposedly you would lose too much money that day.

Despite whatever precautions they may boast, these formulas still try to beat the market—and end up stuck in the same dead-ends as active management. This happens because in retaining some prediction, these approaches also retain some unnecessary risk.[78]

To avoid these pitfalls, you must choose your copilot with care. If you pick up any hint that he is projecting into the future, you're dealing with a hare. That doesn't mean he is trying to trick you, or that he doesn't believe in his predictions. But what assurance do you have that he won't be wrong? None whatsoever! And when he gets it wrong, you join the ranks of the 70% who lose.

So you have to be vigilant. You have to clearly understand how a passive manager operates before you can trust him. Only then can you let him advise you, motivate you, and encourage you—while you remain in control of your investments.

---

75   See technical note, "Stock picking." , page 83
76   See technical note, "Index management vs. passive management." , page 141
77   See technical note, "Market timing." , page 85
78   See technical note, "Unnecessary risks." , page 131

The Alluring Promises of Active Management

One of active management's most powerful tactics is communication. Its influence lies in large part in the enticing image it crafts. Marketing thus plays an indispensable role. It's among the major expenses of a bank, financed by the hundreds of billions taken each year in commissions.[79] Thanks to marketing, banks give their speculative recommendations a seemingly logical spin, enabling them to sell more financial products and persuade more clients to entrust them with their money.

In active investing, the manager can't rely on facts to convince his clients. To mask the random, uncertain nature of his predictions, he has no choice but to play up the emotional aspect, which fuels stress, and the phantasmagorical aspect, which fuels dreams. These two aspects combine to incite the investor to change his positions. It's not in the manager's interest for investments to remain static so he tirelessly pushes for buying and selling. All while wielding his sole argument: that these adjustments are the only effective way to manage a portfolio. They become a "necessary turbulence" that can't be backed up by any certainty, reason, or research.

> "Ignore market timers, Wall Street strategists, technical analysts, and bozo journalists who make market predictions. Admit to your therapist that you can't beat the market."
>
> **Jonathan Clements**
> **Financial reporter**

Unable to justify their actions by simple logic, some financiers use sensationalism to impress the public. Boasting of his company's merits, Lloyd Blankfein, CEO of Goldman Sachs, one of the most prestigious banking firms on the planet (and likewise one of the most profitable for its directors), claims to be "doing God's work."[80] Such blatant provocation enters the collective unconscious and, ironically, works miracles. Thus, without any demonstration, active management furthers its own myth, the golden aura that "gives faith" to millions of investors.

79
- Kenneth R. French, "The Cost of Active Investing." *Journal of Finance* (April 2008), http://ssrn.com/abstract=1105775
- Mark Hulbert. "Can You Beat the Market? It's a $100 Billion Question." *New York Times*, 09.03.2008.

80   John Arlidge. "I'm Doing God's Work: Meet Mister Goldman Sachs." *Sunday Times, 08.11.2009.*

Even if you would never fall for such aggressive rhetoric, you have to watch out for the more measured "demonstrations" that are equally deceptive. To legitimize their profits and methods, certain hares won't hesitate to drop the names of active investing's rare winners and claim success by association. They will take as an example someone like Peter Lynch[81] or Marc Faber,[82] those uncontested but unique talents whose investing prowess has marked the history of finance. Thus they assert, with no basis in fact, that active management presents the only solution for growing a portfolio—thereby fomenting the desire to "beat the market."

A Silent Revolution

Passive management is a "silent revolution." For almost forty years,[83] this philosophy has been discreetly but drastically reshaping the world of finance. Scientifically conducted research revealed the flaws of active management (the efficiency of the markets,[84] the underperformance of active managers, etc.) and then found solutions. As these rifts opened, the most perceptive institutional leaders recognized that it was in their interest to switch to passive investment; with their move, 15% of the world's wealth came to be managed passively.[85] Today, even private portfolios are beginning to lean toward these "subversive" principles.

It sometimes seems that the world's stock exchanges are overrun with hares, but that's not the case. PepsiCo, Boeing, AT&T, Yale University, Kellogg's, the city of Seattle—the list of institutions that have adopted passive management goes on and on. Contrary to what some would have us believe, these managers aren't revolutionaries doing battle with the financial system; rather, they are clear-sighted economists who decided to reconsider the way to manage their money.

81   Peter Lynch was director of the Magellan Fund (Fidelity Investments) from 1977 to 1990. He is considered one of the most talented managers of his time, having directed the Magellan Fund with great success over this long period. The fund went from $20 million in 1977 to $13 billion in 1990, when he retired. Since then he has written several best-selling books.

82   Marc Faber, called "Doctor Doom," is a Swiss investment analyst and entrepreneur. He is considered one of the gurus of finance. His nonconformist views and alternative investment philosophies are often cited in the financial press.

83   See technical note, "The history of passive management." , page 145

84   See technical note, "The efficient market hypothesis." , page 147

85   Interview of John Bogle by Heather Bell. "Active vs. Passive." *Journal of Indexes,* March/April 2009, http://www.indexuniverse.com/publications/journalofindexes/joi-articles/5426-active-vs-passive.html

The passive management philosophy, too, could boast of its prestigious names and successes, but it doesn't need emotional ploys or sensational pitches in order to convince. This "silent revolution" simply appeals to good sense.

Indeed, our tortoise could also play the game of exploiting the biggest names in active management on the planet—and once again she would be the winner, as paradoxical as that might seem.

Among the stars of the financial world, the extraordinary Warren Buffett stands out and cites his mentor Benjamin Graham: *"You're neither right nor wrong because other people agree with you. You're right because your facts are right and your reasoning is right—and that's the only thing that makes you right. And if your facts and reasoning are right, you don't have to worry about anybody else."* [86]

An eminently respected figure, Buffett is regularly held up as an example by promoters of active management—in particular those who are also detractors of passive management. "The Sage of Omaha," as he is known, has become a quasi-magical reference evoked to encourage investors to place bets and to orient their investments toward this or that product, this or that method.

In fact, this finance guru is an unequivocal tortoise ambassador. Not only has Buffett made a bet that no hedge fund manager will be able to outperform the market over a ten-year period,[87] but furthermore he advises his investors to turn to passive investing if they don't want to get caught up in the hare's fierce race.[88]

In other words, given that not everyone can outperform like Warren Buffet, and because an efficient market makes the race pointless,[89] if you want to invest with peace of mind, don't be led astray by hares who rattle off prestigious names in their spectacularly substanceless speeches. Take the more effective and secure route of passive management.

---

86   Interview with Warren Buffett by Julia Boorstin. "The Best Advice I Ever Got." *Fortune Magazine*, 21.03.2005.

87   http://www.longbets.org/362

88   This is essentially what he advises in the annual meetings held for all his investors in Omaha. See Berkshire Hathaway's annual report for 2005, 18 http://www.berkshirehathaway.com/2005ar/2005ar.pdf

89   See technical note, "The efficient market hypothesis." , page 147

A Cure within Everyone's Reach

The investor's persistent unease with the financial world stems from three sources: a sketchy grasp of how the market works, the apparent sophistication of managers, and the abuses committed by financial institutions. But it doesn't have to be that way. As we have shown in this book, the fog surrounding wealth management can be lifted.

Looking after one's investments requires understanding the situation, which is the first step to taking back control. As with the child's nighttime terrors, all that is needed is to "turn on the light" and locate your familiar reference points within this space— that is, within the parameters surrounding your capital.

As we write this, passive management celebrates forty years of existence. However, up to now it has been largely confined to the institutional investors. This situation is quickly changing, spurred by enormous regulatory pressures for greater transparency and by growing demands from private investors.

This book doesn't propose any miracle solution. Our goal was rather to lead investors to step back from traditional management and take a look at the whole picture.

And so, armed with reason and critical judgment, every person can begin the process leading to investment peace of mind. Accompanied by their copilot, they can build a financial plan that truly corresponds to their needs. That plan is then transformed into a passive portfolio, completely free of the stress of speculation and loss of control. Market turbulence is turned to the investor's advantage. It is a commonsense process that is also supported by scientific research, and that will restore your objectivity and confidence in investing.

Knowing *the story your banker will never tell you*, it is the juncture for you to take action. You can either call your financial advisor to let him know how you want him to work for you, or look for the right co-pilot to guide you with your investments. You can also seek a second opinion from an independent and objective expert to assess whether you are well positioned to reach your objectives and ensure you have considered all options before taking your decision.

The time has come for you to *heal your investments*.

Words of Thanks

To Sarah Genequand, without whom this book would never have seen the light of day.

To our clients, who were the first to give us their trust. Open to new concepts, they also had the critical judgment to question the assertions of a whole industry. Our regular meetings with them taught us a great deal, helping to transform our finance jargon into transparent and understandable speech. Their enthusiasm and encouragement is what inspired us to write this book.

To our wives, Andreia and Annelie, and our mothers, Magda and Ulrica, who supported us with great patience and strength.

To our early readers, whose critiques were invaluable: Malak Poppovic, Françoise Wicht, Gérard Fatio, Alan Hughes, Raphaële Arnbäck, Philippe Roch, Alexandre Constantinescu, Alexis Zottos, Jean Brunel, Michel Oltramare, Jacques Boissonnas, and Grégoire Worko; to those who offered their support: Candice Bal, Véronique Bühlmann, Lygia, Marcela Lima Tomaz, Sonia Santos, Nicole Schwab, Majid El Sohl, Lise Moeller, and Charles Monney; and finally, to all those who wished to remain anonymous.

Technical Notes

The various levels of fees[90]

The total cost of an actively managed investment portfolio ranges from 2% to 5% per year. Some managers, however, may quote costs as low as 0.5% to 1.5%. [91] The difference can be explained by the various layers of cost that cut into the portfolio's return.

Management fee: the manager's fee for his or her work and advice often runs between 0.5% and 1.5% a year.

Custody fee: what a bank charges for storing assets in its vault and for handling asset accounting (payment of dividends, stock splits and mergers, etc.). These fees are usually between 0.1% and 0.6% of the total value of the account per year.

Transaction fee: each time a traded asset is bought or sold, the cost of the execution must be paid. Depending on the transaction, this can be up to 5% of the amount involved.

Kickback: banks often entrust certain transactions to agents and pass the agents' fees on to their clients.

Forex spread: every operation involving a currency exchange (for example, buying euros with dollars) involves a cost. The "spread"—the difference between the market cost and the exchange cost—is billed to the client.

---

90   See technical note, "The impact of compound interest on fees and performance", page 125.
91
– Warren Giles. "Rich Pumped for Fees in Banking Conflict of Interest." *Business Week*, 24.03.2010.
– Lipper Offshore Fund Charges Report. Quarterly Edition, January 2010.
– Christian Nolterieke. "Cut the Costs of Wealth Management." 28.05.2009, http://www.myprivatebank-ing.com/report/wealth-guide-2

– William F. Sharpe. "The Arithmetic of Active Management." *Financial Analysts Journal* 47:1 (1991): 7-9.

Performance fee: some managers charge this only if they produce positive results.

Securities lending: when a financial institution holds traded assets (stocks, bonds, etc.) for its clients, it is not unusual for another financial actor to want to "rent" them. (It is as if a customer stored his car in a garage and the garage owner rented it out when the customer wasn't using it.) Some lending institutions pass along all of the "rental" to their clients, but most keep a large share of it.

Financial products fees: for example funds of hedge funds often charge investors between 2% and 5% per year. These products are among the most profitable for the financial industry.

Commission on a structured product: Due to their lack of transparency, it is often hard to measure the total amount of commissions and fees collected on structured financial products. Such fees can easily amount to 4%.

Stock picking: choosing among stocks

This management method consists of picking one or a number of stocks from among all those traded on the market. In theory, your purchase of a stock should reflect the perception of a potential increase in value and potentially better performance than the market average. Conversely, in the case of a sale, your choice should allow you to discard losing stocks—the ones that will underperform the market average or that present a large downside risk. Several different approaches can help determine which shares to buy or sell.[92]

Picking the right stock is a real challenge, as this example from the *Wall Street Journal* shows. In February 2005[93], the newspaper asked various analysts to pick the ten best and the ten worst companies from the S&P 500—a reference index composed of the 500 largest U.S. companies—for the current year. [94]

Here is what happened: In 2005 the S&P 500 rose 9%, and the stock prices of the ten best companies identified by the experts improved by 13%. This would tend to prove that the analysts' work added value to the process. In the same year, however, the stock prices of the ten worst companies, as named by those same experts, rose by 19%! The conclusion reached? In spite of their work, the analysts didn't generate any added value. The fact is that the movement of stocks is unpredictable,[95] so it is impossible to pick the stocks that will rise or fall. [96]

---

92   See technical note, "Types of financial analysis." , page 91
93   Gregory Zuckerman. "Love'em! Hate'em!" *Wall Street Journal*, 07.02.2005.
94   We use the S&P 500 as a reference because it's the oldest, and the one most used in American academic research.
95   "The price of a traded asset is unpredictable." Paul A Samuelson, "Proof that Properly Anticipated Prices Fluctuate Randomly." *Industrial Management Review* 6:2 (1965), 41.
96   See technical note, "The efficient market hypothesis." , page 147

Remember, too, that stock picking comes at a cost. With each buy or sell order, you not only face the risk of error but must also pay the cost of the transaction. [97]

Market timing: tactical asset allocation

Market timing is an investment method by which investors adjust their market exposure depending on the markets' movements. Based on an analysis of the current situation, they choose the asset classes that they feel offer the greatest potential for gain at a particular moment. Various analytical methods determine whether the economic conditions are favorable or not.[98] For example, in times of crisis it is better to hold bonds rather than stocks.

Choosing the right time to invest[99] is, however, just as risky as choosing the right stock.[100] And in addition to assuming the risk of error you must also pay the transaction costs.[101]

A study by the market research firm DALBAR[102] reveals that investors who moved from one asset to another missed about one-third of the profits earned by the assets. The study showed that between 1984 and 1997 the average U.S. stock investor got an annual return of 6.7%, whereas the S&P 500, an index composed of the 500 largest U.S. companies, climbed 17.1%!

> "Only liars manage to always be out during bad times and in during good times."
>
> **Bernard Baruch**
> **Economic Advisor to**
> **W. Wilson & F. Roosevelt**

---

98   See technical note, "Types of financial analysis." , page 91
99   See technical note, "The efficient market hypothesis." , page 147
100   See technical note, "Stock-picking." , page 83
101   See technical note, "The various levels of fees." , page 81
102   Larry E Swedroe. *What Wall Street Doesn't Want You to Know.* New York: Truman Talley Books/ Dutton, 2001: 145.

Manager selection: follow leaders of the past

There are two kinds of financial managers:

A wealth manager manages other people's financial assets. He or she may be independent or work for a bank. How the managed accounts perform is not a matter of public record.

A fund manager manages one or more investment funds. How those funds perform is public information and accessible to everyone. Some funds are even listed on the market.

Choosing the right manager involves identifying the ones who will produce the best results among all the fund managers on the planet. To determine which funds should be bought or sold, bankers and other financial experts (including wealth managers) spend a lot of energy analyzing the funds' past performance and evaluating their investment strategies.

Yet all the studies, without exception, show that it is impossible to identify in advance the managers or funds that will outperform the markets.[103] Why? Simply because all of them use either stock picking or market timing to try to beat the market.[104]

By way of illustration, let's look at the performance of the ten best British funds over a five-year period (see the chart on the next page). Only two funds continued to beat the market during the five following years. Take the funds of any other market in the United States, Europe, or Asia, and you will find similar ratios.

---

103   See technical note, "The efficient market hypothesis." , page 147
104   See technical note, "Stock-picking" and "market timing." , page 83 and 85

WHO KEEPS ON WINNING ?

FUND NAME	JAN 99 TO DEC 03		JAN 04 TO DEC 08	
	RANK OVER 149 FUNDS	PERF. VS MARKETS	RANK OVER 239 FUNDS	PERF. VS MARKETS
Rathbone Special Sits Inc	1	ABOVE	239	BELOW
Gam UK Diversified Inc	2	ABOVE	112	BELOW
Fidelity Special Situations	3	ABOVE	7	ABOVE
Cavendish Opportunities RTL	4	ABOVE	236	BELOW
Artemis UK Growth	5	ABOVE	172	BELOW
Malborough UK Equity Growth	6	ABOVE	229	BELOW
Solus UK Special Situations Inc	7	ABOVE	182	BELOW
Schoder Recovery Inc	8	ABOVE	61	BELOW
Blackrock UK Special Sits A Inc	9	ABOVE	24	ABOVE
Artemis Capital	10	ABOVE	161	BELOW

Source: Morningstar

In addition, a recent S&P (SPIVA) study[105] shows that funds with poor past performance have a statistically better chance of succeeding in the future than the funds that performed the best.

It is important to note that besides the risk of error, choosing managers also has a direct cost. After you finance the research and analysis, you still have to pay the cost of transactions.[106]

---

105   Standard & Poor's "Does Past Performance Matter?" http://img.en25.com/Web/
StandardandPoors/PersistenceScorecard_June10_Final.pdf, June 2010
106   See technical note, "The various levels of fees." , page 81

Types of financial analysis

Macroeconomic analysis, also called top-down analysis, consists of following the broad movements of a sector or a country. The analysis studies the growth potential of the various sectors or countries so as to identify which ones are likely to perform well and which aren't worth investing in. The conclusions of such analysis are typically formulated this way: "China has fantastic growth potential," or "The pharmaceutical sector is recession proof," or "Gold is a safe asset."

Fundamental analysis, also called bottom-up analysis, consists in carefully studying a company traded on the market and judging its potential for growth or its resistance to recession. To support their opinions, analysts study the company's management, its sector activity (economic analysis), competition (comparative analysis), financial solidity (accounting analysis), etc. They gather and feed a great deal of data into prediction models to determine the best investment. Such an analysis might recommend buying Microsoft rather than Apple, for example.

Quantitative analysis uses probability-derived financial mathematics to refine models that allow analysts to identify the best investments. This approach is based on the belief that the market's past behavior will be repeated in the future. Some funds are managed entirely according to quantitative models. Quantitative analysts, nicknamed "quants," have backgrounds in both mathematics and finance.

Technical analysis consists in studying stock charts and judging market sentiment in order to anticipate market movements. For example, a given stock may have suffered more than its competitors; investors have lost all confidence in it, so you shouldn't touch it. Or to the contrary, this other company has reversed its decline and investors are paying more attention to it, making this the time to buy.

"Star manager" behavior analysis: practitioners of this technique try to copy the investment methods of managers who have produced exceptional results in the past.

Conventional wisdom may influence investors' behavior to a certain extent. Here is a sample adage: "Sell in May and go away" means sell your stocks in the spring and go on vacation!

Whatever the method chosen, there are two kinds of "producers" of analyses:

- **Sell-side analysis** is produced by stockbrokers. These analysts are specialists and generally focus on a small number of companies or sectors. Their income depends on their clients' transactions with the stocks they recommend, so it is obviously in their interest to maximize the number of trades.
- **Buy-side analysis** is produced by managers who are in charge of investing money. Because they often rely on a number of sell-side analyses, these managers cover a much larger number of companies or sectors. This in turn gives them a broader overall view of the market.

Few managers beat the markets

A tiny minority of managers beat them several years in a row

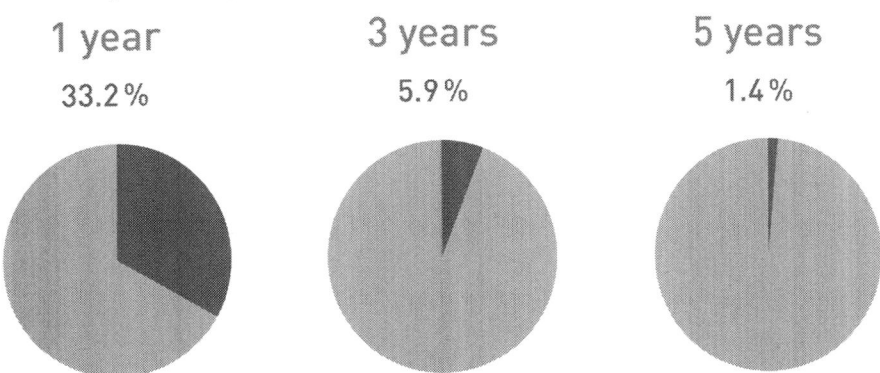

1 year	3 years	5 years
33.2%	5.9%	1.4%

Source: University of Chicago, 2004 to 2008, on 2,619 funds

The three pie charts above represent the number of managers who beat the market over periods of one, three, and five years.

What are the chances of success when choosing a manager?

All the studies[107] show that in the short term about 66% of investors do worse than the market average. Over longer periods, the proportion of

107   Examples of studies:
– Prof. L. Barras, O. Scaillet, and R. Wermers. Swiss Finance Institute. "False Discoveries in Mutual Fund Performance: Measuring Luck in Estimated Alphas," in *Research Paper Series* N°08-18, 2008.
– Andy Baker. *The Economist*, Special Report, "Money for Old Hope." 01.03.2008.
– Alfred Cowles, III. "Can Stock Market Forecasters Forecast?" *Econometria* 1:3 (1933): 309–324.
– DALBAR. Study Shows Market Timers Lose Their Money, press release, April 2004.
– James L. Davis. "Mutual Fund Performance and Manager Style." *Financial Analyst Journal* 57:1 (2001): 19–27.
– Eugene F. Fama and Kenneth R. French. "Luck versus Skill in the Cross Section of Mutual Fund Returns." *Journal of Finance* (December 2009)

investors who beat the market gets even smaller, because it is rare for winners to keep winning year after year.

As the figure shows, managers on average are not able to beat the market. The figure describes the performance of U.S. funds over a period of fifteen years.

– Michael Jensen. "The Performance of Mutual Funds in the Period 1945–1964." *Journal of Finance* 23:2 (1967): 389–416.
– Pat Regnier. "Can You Outsmart the Market?" *Fortune Magazine*, 21.12.2009.
– Jason Zweig, "Why Many Investors Keep Fooling Themselves." *Wall Street Journal*, 16.01.2010.
– Standard & Poor's. "Standard & Poor's Indices Versus Active Funds Scorecard, Year End 2008." 20.04.2009, http://www.standardandpoors.com/indices/spiva/en/us

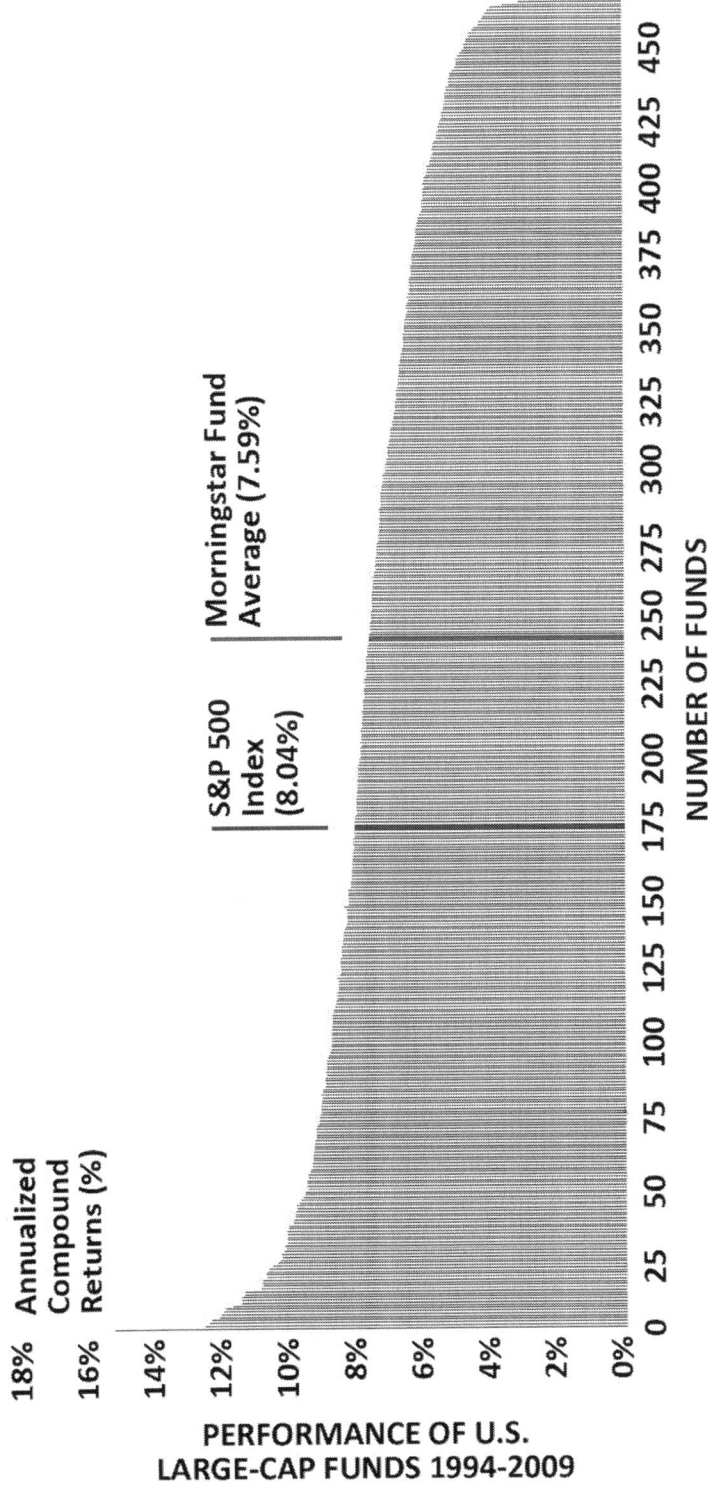

PERFORMANCE OF U.S.
LARGE-CAP FUNDS 1994-2009

Each gray line represents the 1994–2009 performance of a U.S. fund trying to beat the S&P 500, which is the index of the 500 largest U.S. companies. The bold vertical line on the left represents the performance of the market (S&P 500). The bold vertical line on the right represents the average of all of the funds (Morningstar Fund Average).

This graph shows that:

- The Morningstar Fund Average falls in the middle because it represents the average performance of all funds.
- The Morningstar Fund Average is always below the Index (S&P 500).
- Some 64 % of managers did less well than the market (64% of the gray lines are to the right of the S&P 500 line).

Why weren't most of the managers able to beat the market?

The short answer is that as a group, investors can't earn more than the market produces.

To understand why, think of a high-school class where the average grade is 7 out of 10. If one student gets 10/10, one of his or her classmates must obviously have gotten 4/10, since (10 + 4)/2 = 7, which is the class average. No matter what happens, it is impossible for all the students to get 10/10 if the average is 7/10.

By definition, the market represents the investor average (like the class average). When one investor sells a stock, another investor buys it. That means that if the market rises 10% and one investor gets a return of 11%, some other investor must be getting less than 10%. Investing is a zero-sum game: each time one investor makes a profit, another suffers a loss. If some people were lucky enough to hold only stocks that outperformed the market as a whole, others must have held stocks that didn't do as well.

average

| 50 % | 50 % |

When confronted with this 50-50 split, you may well wonder: how is it possible that financial professionals as a group do worse than the market? This is where the comparison with the high-school class ends. That is because with investments you also have to take into account the impact of fees, such as management and transaction fees.[108]

If we add up all the fees, and assume they come to 2%, for example, investors who manage to beat the market and earn an 11% return before costs actually get only 9% (11% − 2% = 9%), a return below the market average.

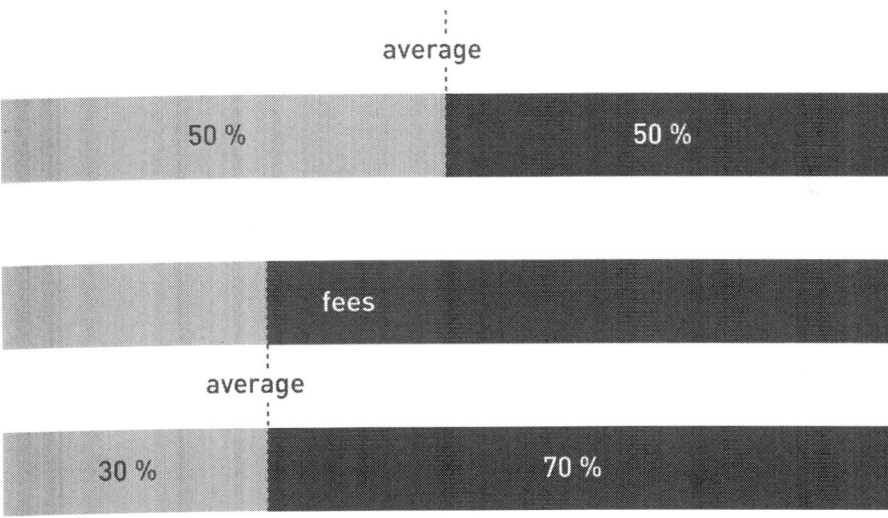

"Core" and "satellite" portfolios

This technique is often used by institutional investors to divide assets into two distinct pots.

- The "core" pot is the portion of assets you can't or don't want to risk. In general, this part is invested in classic assets—bonds or blue-chip stocks. Depending on the proportion of stocks and bonds, this portfolio can fluctuate, of course.
- The "satellite" pot is invested more aggressively. This is the speculative part of the portfolio. For example, it might be invested in an option whose value could increase tenfold or, in the worst case, could fall to zero.

Tips on choosing a good copilot

Even though the methods discussed in this book have existed for more than forty years and are widely used in the institutional world, there are few professionals in continental Europe who work with Individual investors and use these methods. Finding the right financial advisor to guide you is an important step. To be most helpful, he or she must understand your personal situation, as well as your hopes and dreams. It is essential that this be someone you feel comfortable with—someone you trust. If you wish to convert your portfolio and are looking for a suitable advisor, some of the suggestions below will be useful.

- You must be sure the advisor shares your **investment philosophy**. You can't convert your portfolio to passive management if your advisor is an active manager.
- Be sure to **separate investment advice from asset deposit**. Never seek investment advice from the same institution where your assets are deposited. The conflict of interest would be too great, and the situation immediately puts you in an inferior position.
- **Advisor remuneration.** Make sure your manager is paid only by you, and receives no fees or kickbacks from the funds or custody institutions that he or she uses. These issues should be specifically covered in the management agreement.
- **The manager.** Check out his or her training, professional qualifications, and experience.

Here are some questions to ask prospective managers:

- Do they think they can beat the financial markets? If so, how and why? If they are wrong in their investment advice, how much would a mistake cost you?

- What would they do if the market crashes? (Bear in mind that a true passive manager doesn't use market timing.[109] He remains invested all the time, so as to be able to profit from market recoveries).
- Ask them how they choose investment vehicles and what criteria they use.

In conclusion, a good manager should be able to guide you, help you make **rational decisions**, and eliminate emotional considerations. You, in turn, should make sure your personal situation defines your portfolio choice, instead of having market movements influence your choice of investments.

Sources of financial advice:

- *The Internet* is a wonderful source of information, where you can pick up a lot of help. If you put in the time, you can educate yourself in passive management and apply the technique at very low cost. The disadvantage of relying on the Internet is that you are alone in facing the markets and may be tempted to change your behavior when times get tough.
- *A consultant* will help you master the basics more quickly and provide good company during difficult times. Seasoned investors who want to manage their fortune themselves can also benefit from using a consultant. Make sure that the advisor gets no other income than what the two of you agree on.
- *A specialist in passive management* is the most effective solution. This guarantees you access to all the subtleties of passive management, including institutional funds that are closed to the public and to banks. Be absolutely sure that your advisor receives no kickbacks and stipulate this in writing in the management agreement.

---

109   See technical note, "Market timing." , page 85

Setting your goals and creating a financial plan

E very reasonable investment decision should begin with a "business plan." If one of your friends asked you to invest $10,000 in his new restaurant, you would expect him to submit a budget, along with projected sales figures and the potential profitability of his business. When you entrust your savings to a banker, however, you almost never receive such a plan.

Most traditional managers will talk about risk profile and ask you whether you're more on the conservative or the aggressive side. This discussion might last only ten minutes; at best, an hour. Unfortunately, this approach has two major flaws:

- Investors don't have a single risk profile; they have several, each corresponding to a specific goal.[110]
- The failure to plan investments according to precise goals leads to frequent transactions in response to market fluctuations. All this back-and-forth usually proves counterproductive in terms of returns.

Good financial planning is relatively simple. There are three steps:

1. Define your goals and the means to achieve them.
2. Divide your assets into "compartments," each keyed to a specific goal.

110   David Bogoslaw. "Retirement: Goal-based Investing Gains Traction." *Bloomberg Businessweek,* 18.08.2009.

3. Make sure your goals are feasible with the means at your
   disposal.

1. Define your goals

Let's say you have $100,000, and you want to do two things:

- You would like to remodel your house next summer, which will
  cost $50,000.
- You have two children to put through college fifteen years from
  now, and you will need $40,000 for each.

That means you have $100,000 right now, and you will need to have
$130,000 to meet your goals. Are your goals feasible? Probably so.
Let's figure it out.

2. Divide your assets into "compartments"

The money for the remodeling represents a low-risk profile, because you will have to pay the bills in the very near future. On the other
hand, the money for college has a higher risk profile: you won't need
that money for fifteen years, so the losses you may incur in the mean-
time will be less significant overall. In this example, then, you have two
very different risk profiles.

This means your assets should be divided into two "compartments":

- $50,000 with the least risk possible
- $50,000 with a certain amount of risk

So how should they be invested? Considering the information given
in our technical notes "Stocks and bonds" and "Creating value: stocks"
(below), we could, for example:

- Put the money for remodeling in short-term, high-quality bonds
  in U.S. dollars.
- Invest the amount set aside for college in a portfolio consisting of
  60%world-wide stocks and 40% short-term, high-quality bonds
  in U.S. dollars.

3. Make sure your goals are feasible

Will you be able to reach these two goals?

As far as the house is concerned, you know that bonds are the best way to ensure that your money will be available when the remodeling bills arrive.

As far as your children's college education, you have no crystal ball, but you know that in the long term, stocks yield higher returns than bonds and fifteen years is a relatively long time. In this case, your best reference point is the past. You know that a portfolio consisting of 60% stocks and 40% bonds yields, on average, a 7% return. At that rate, in fifteen years your $50,000 would become $128,927, which is more than what you need. You must also be aware, however, that in bad years such a portfolio can lose up to 30% of its value. Are you prepared to accept losses on that scale?[111]

This method in no way guarantees that you will reach the precise goals you have set. It does, however, give you the best likelihood of reaching them—and with the least possible stress.

Now let's suppose that after running the numbers, you find that your goals would be hard to reach. Say you wanted $200,000 instead of $40,000 for each of your children fifteen years from now. Even with 100% in stocks, after fifteen years, your $50,000 would come to only $189,874, leaving you $210,000 short of your goal. What can you do now? There are three options:

- Revise your goals to a lower amount.
- Save more money to add to your compartments.
- Turn to speculating, taking thoughtless risks, putting everything on the line—in other words, going back to active management.

Your copilot will guide you to the right choice.

---

111   See the technical notes, "Stocks and bonds," "Creating value: stocks," and "The impact of compound interest on fees and performance." , pages 111, 123 and 125

From academic research to passive management

Passive management is based on dozens of certainties uncovered during scientific and academic research, some of which was awarded Nobel Prizes in economics. Here is a summary of major historical academic research done on the financial markets.[112]

1950. Conventional Wisdom circa 1950

Analyze securities one by one. Focus on picking winners. Concentrate holdings to maximize returns.

Broad diversification is considered undesirable.

"Once you attain competency, diversification is undesirable. One or two, or at most three or four, securities should be bought. Competent investors will never be satisfied beating the averages by a few small percentage points."

Gerald M. Loeb, *The Battle for Investment Survival*, 1935

1952. Diversification and Portfolio Risk

Harry Markowitz, Nobel Prize in Economics, 1990

Diversification reduces risk.

Assets evaluated not by individual characteristics but by their effect on a portfolio.

An optimal portfolio can be constructed to maximize return for a given standard deviation.

1958. The Role of Stocks

James Tobin, Nobel Prize in Economics, 1981

Separation Theorem:

1. Form portfolio of risky assets.

2. Temper risk by lending and borrowing.

Shifts focus from security selection to portfolio structure.

"Liquidity Preference as Behavior Toward Risk." *Review of Economic Studies,* February 1958.

1961. Investments and Capital Structure

Merton Miller and Franco Modigliani, Nobel Prizes in Economics, 1985 and 1990

Theorem related corporate finance to returns.

A firm's value is unrelated to its dividend policy

1964. Single-Factor Asset Pricing Risk/Return Model

William Sharpe, Nobel Prize in Economics, 1990

Capital Asset Pricing Model:

Theoretical model defines risk as volatility relative to market.

A stock's cost of capital (the investor's expected return) is proportional to the stock's risk relative to the entire stock universe.

Theoretical model for evaluating the risk and expected return of securities and portfolios.

1965. Behavior of Securities Prices

Paul Samuelson, MIT, Nobel Prize in Economics, 1970

Market prices are the best estimates of value.

Price changes follow random patterns. Future share prices are unpredictable.

"Proof that Properly Anticipated Prices Fluctuate Randomly,"

Industrial Management Review, Spring 1965

1966. Efficient Markets Hypothesis

Eugene F. Fama, University of Chicago

Extensive research on stock price patterns.

Develops "Efficient Markets Hypothesis," which asserts that prices reflect values and information accurately and quickly. It is difficult if not impossible to capture returns in excess of market returns without taking greater than market levels of risk.

Investors cannot identify superior stocks using fundamental information or price patterns.

1968. First Major Study of Manager Performance

Michael Jensen, 1965; A.G. Becker Corporation, 1968

First studies of mutual funds (Jensen) and of institutional plans (A.G. Becker Corp.) indicate active managers underperform indexes.

Becker Corp. gives rise to consulting industry with creation of "Green Book" performance tables comparing results to benchmarks.

1971. The Birth of Index Funds

John McQuown, Wells Fargo Bank, 1971;

Rex Sinquefield, American National Bank, 1973

Banks develop the first passive S&P 500 Index funds. Years later, Sinquefield co-chairs Dimensional, and McQuown sits on its Board.

1972. Options Pricing Model

Fischer Black and Myron Scholes, University of Chicago; Robert Merton,

Harvard University; Nobel Prize in Economics, 1997

The development of the Options Pricing Model allows new ways to segment, quantify, and manage risk.

The model spurs the development of a market for alternative investments.

1975. A Major Plan First Commits to Indexing

New York Telephone Company invests $40 million in an S&P 500 Index fund.

The first major plan to index.

Helps launch the era of indexed investing.

"Fund spokesmen are quick to point out you can't buy the market averages. It's time the public could."

Burton G. Malkiel, *A Random Walk Down Wall Street, 1973 ed.*

Creation of Vanguard Index 500 Fund

John Bogle, Vanguard

First index fund opened to private investors

1977. Database of Securities Prices since 1926

Roger Ibbotson and Rex Sinquefield,

Stocks, Bonds, Bills, and Inflation

An extensive returns database for multiple asset classes is first developed and will become one of the most widely used investment databases.

The first extensive, empirical basis for making asset allocation decisions changes the way investors build portfolios.

1981. The Size Effect

Rolf Banz, University of Chicago

Analyzed NYSE stocks, 1926-1975.

Finds that, in the long term, small companies have higher expected returns than large companies and behave differently.

1984. Variable maturity bond strategy

Eugene F. Fama

With no prediction of interest rates, Eugene Fama develops a method of shifting maturities that identifies optimal positions on the fixed income yield curve.

"The Information in the Term Structure"

Journal of Financial Economics 13:4 (December 1984) : pp 509-528

1990. Nobel Prize Recognizes Modern Finance

Economists who shaped the way we invest are recognized, emphasizing the role of science in finance.

William Sharpe for the Capital Asset Pricing Model.

Harry Markowitz for portfolio theory.

Merton Miller for work on the effect of firms' capital structure and dividend policy on their prices.

1992. Multifactor Asset Pricing Model and Value Effect

Eugene Fama and Kenneth French, University of Chicago

Improves on the single-factor asset pricing model (CAPM).

Identifies market, size, and "value" factors in returns.

Develops the three-factor asset pricing model, an invaluable asset allocation and portfolio analysis tool.

1995. Size effect on international markets

Steven L. Heston, K. Geert Rousenhorst and Roberto E. Wessels.

Demonstrate that small companies produce on average higher returns on twelve international markets

"The structure of International Stock Returns and the Integration of Capital Markets." *Journal of Empirical Finance* 2:3 (September 1995):pp.173-197

2006. Equity strategy

Eugene F. Fama and Kenneth R. French

By overweighting small and value stocks in relationship to their weight in the market, portfolio turnover and fees can be reduced.

"Migration," CRSP Working Paper no. 614, Center for Research in Security Prices, University of Chicago, February 2007

Stocks and bonds

A company has two sources of market financing:

- It can increase its capital by issuing **stocks**.
- It can borrow money by issuing **bonds**.

A share of stock represents part of a company's capital. Stockholders are thereby owners, and the value of their investment will fluctuate along with the company's financial developments. A stock's price varies and has no upper or lower limit.

A bond is a loan. For two main reasons its price fluctuates much less than a share of stock:

- The bond's yield—the interest paid by the company, which represents the cost of "renting" money—guarantees a floor price for the bond.
- Bondholders are always in line ahead of stockholders to be compensated in case of bankruptcy. As a result, although bondholders may recoup their investment, stockholders usually don't.

The graph on the next page illustrates the difference between stocks and bonds in terms of risk and return.

- Look at the lower curve, which represents the movement of high-quality, short-term bonds denominated in Swiss francs. Yield is relatively low and stable, but never negative.
- The upper curve represents the movement of stock markets (25% Swiss, 25% European, and 50% worldwide, with quarterly rebalancing). You can see that stocks gain over the long term, but

that drastic dips occur in some years, with losses of up to 44% of the stocks' value.

Stocks or bonds? Risks or returns?

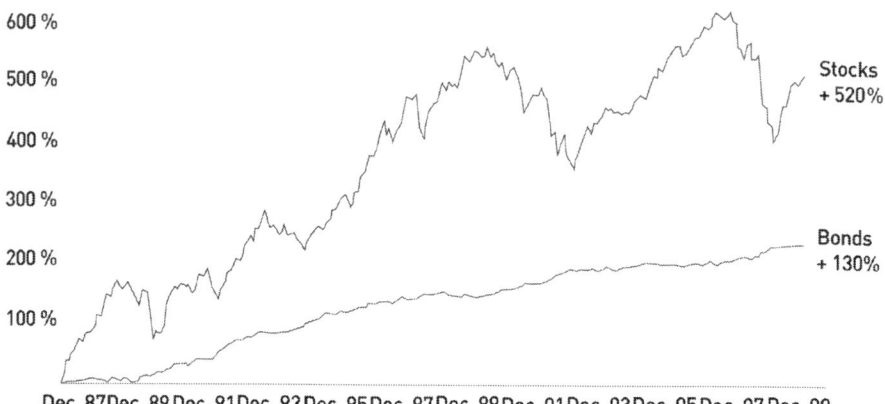

Over 22 years, for each CHF invested	Bonds	Stocks
Amounts in CHF	CHF 2.30	CHF 6.20
Worst year	+0.06%	-44.00%
Sources : MSCI, Citigroup Index		

Dividing a portfolio among financial instruments

Investments fall into two broad categories:

- Fixed income, low-risk instruments with a low return, such as bonds.
- Risky asset, high-risk instruments that can offer substantial gains, such as stocks.

A traditional portfolio might consist of all sorts of financial products, each more sophisticated than the next. Unfortunately, these products are often complicated and expensive; moreover, they lack transparency.

Let's look at a sample traditional portfolio with the following positions:

- Cash in a current account, fiduciary deposits
- Corporate or government bonds
- A bond fund
- A guaranteed capital product
- Individual stocks
- A stock fund
- A real estate fund
- A hedge fund
- Commodities

In contrast, a passive manager will put together a portfolio that is as simple as possible and that lets the investor invest in the entire market (no picking or making subjective choices) for optimal return. To do this, he uses financial products that guarantee maximum diversification at minimum cost.

Under passive management, the traditional portfolio shown above could be divided as follows:

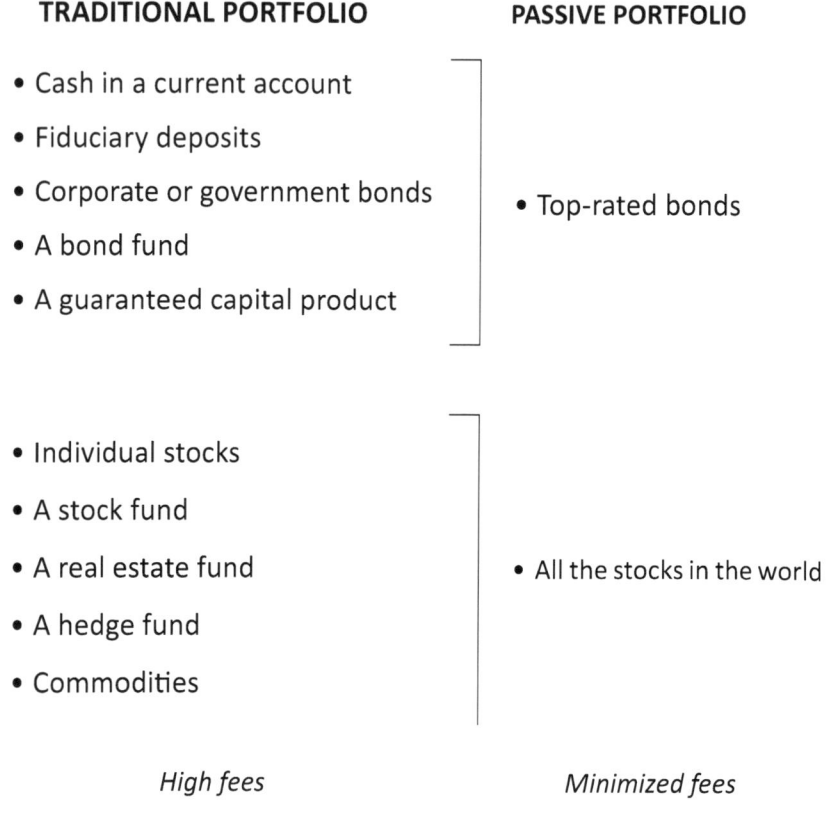

TRADITIONAL PORTFOLIO   PASSIVE PORTFOLIO

- Cash in a current account
- Fiduciary deposits
- Corporate or government bonds   • Top-rated bonds
- A bond fund
- A guaranteed capital product

- Individual stocks
- A stock fund
- A real estate fund   • All the stocks in the world
- A hedge fund
- Commodities

High fees   *Minimized fees*

It is obviously much easier to evaluate risk in the portfolio on the right.

Why it's risky to hold cash

A bank operates a bit like a furniture warehouse. In the simplest terms, it holds two kinds of assets:

- **Investments** (stocks, bonds, funds, etc.) are simply "stored" in the bank's vault. Like furniture, these assets belong to the individual who deposited them, and are not part of the bank's balance sheet—they are accounted for separately. If the bank fails, the customers will recover their goods.
- **Liquid assets** (cash and fiduciary deposits) are carried on the bank's balance sheet. In the furniture warehouse example, this might be money used to pay three years' advance rent. If the warehouse company goes bankrupt, customers can get their furniture back, but not the advance rent they paid. In the case of a bank, money in a checking or savings account is part of the bank's assets and will be paid to creditors in case of bankruptcy.

To reduce bankruptcy risk to depositors, most governments guarantee asset accounts up to a certain amount. In case of bankruptcy, bank customers will only lose the amount that exceeds the guarantee level. During a financial crisis like the one in 2008, savers will often open accounts at several different banks, each for an amount below the government guarantee level.

A simpler alternative would be to invest liquid assets in government bonds, for example.

Why government bonds are the safest investment

A bond represents a loan. The price of the bond fluctuates depending on its term and yield. It also depends on the quality of the bond issuer, that is, on the issuer's ability to repay the loan.

Government bonds work much like the bonds issued by a company.[113] When a government needs money, it issues a bond and repays the loan at a fixed rate of interest over a specified term of years. Unlike a company, however, a government can create money in case of crisis, simply by printing more of it.[114] This means that a government, unlike any other institution, can't go bankrupt in its own currency!

---

113   See technical note, "Stocks and bonds." , page 111
114   While it's true that printing money has negative effects, such as loss of confidence and inflation, the holder of government bonds remains sure to be reimbursed. An investor in Greek bonds denominated in euros is theoretically exposed to debtor risk because even though Greece is a nation, it can't print euros. It would be wiser to choose euro-denominated obligations issued directly by the "money printer," in this case the Central European Bank.

Short-term government bonds in your country's currency

To avoid the uncertainties of forecasting, it is important to put assets that you can't afford to lose in the safest possible investment and to accept a low rate of return[115].

The safest investment is a short-term government bond in its own reference currency[116].

Why?

- A government bond is the safest investment.[117]
- Short terms are also safer, because a long-term bond exposes you to the risk of future inflation and potential loss. For example, if you buy a long-term bond (say, thirty years) with a yield of 3% per year, and inflation hits 5%, the bond will lose value because the 3% interest it pays is less than the rate of inflation. Over

---

115   Risks and rewards are inextricably linked :
- William F. Sharpe. "Capital Asset Prices: A Theory of Market Equilibrium under Conditions of Risk." *Journal of Finance* 19:3 (1964): 425-442.
- Jeremy J. Siegel. *Stocks for the Long Run*. New York : McGraw-Hill, 1998
- Sidney Homer, A History of Interest Rates. New Brunswick, NJ: Rutgers University Press, 1963
- Eugene F. Fama and Kenneth R. French, "The Cross-Section of Expected Stock Returns." *Journal of Finance*, December 1998.
- Eugene F. Fama and Kenneth R. French, "Value versus Growth: The International Evidence." *Journal of Finance*, December 1998.
- Ombudsman des banques suisses. "Rendement élevé égal risque élevé." http://www.bankingombudsman.ch communiqué of 07.07.2009.

116   The reference currency is usually the currency in which the customer spends his money. Suppose a person lives six months a year in the United States and six months in Europe. Ideally he should have two portfolios, one in dollars and the other in euros, with which to pay his expenses in each area.

117   See technical note, "Why government bonds are the safest investment." , page 117

shorter periods (less than three years), the impact of inflation on a bond's value is practically nil.

- By sticking to the reference currency, you avoid any currency exchange risk.[118]

Government bonds and inflation

Let's compare the curves for inflation and U.S. government bonds (see the graph on the next page).

The example chosen covers eighty-three years of history, a period marked by market crashes, world wars, elections, etc.

From 1926 to 2006, inflation—meaning the general rise in prices—turned $1 into $12. In other words, a breakfast that cost one greenback in 1926 costs twelve today.

Over the same time period, short-term U.S. government bonds went from $1 to $21. By reinvesting capital and accumulated interest each year, $1 million would have grown to $21 million, roughly keeping pace with inflation.

January 1926 – December 2009

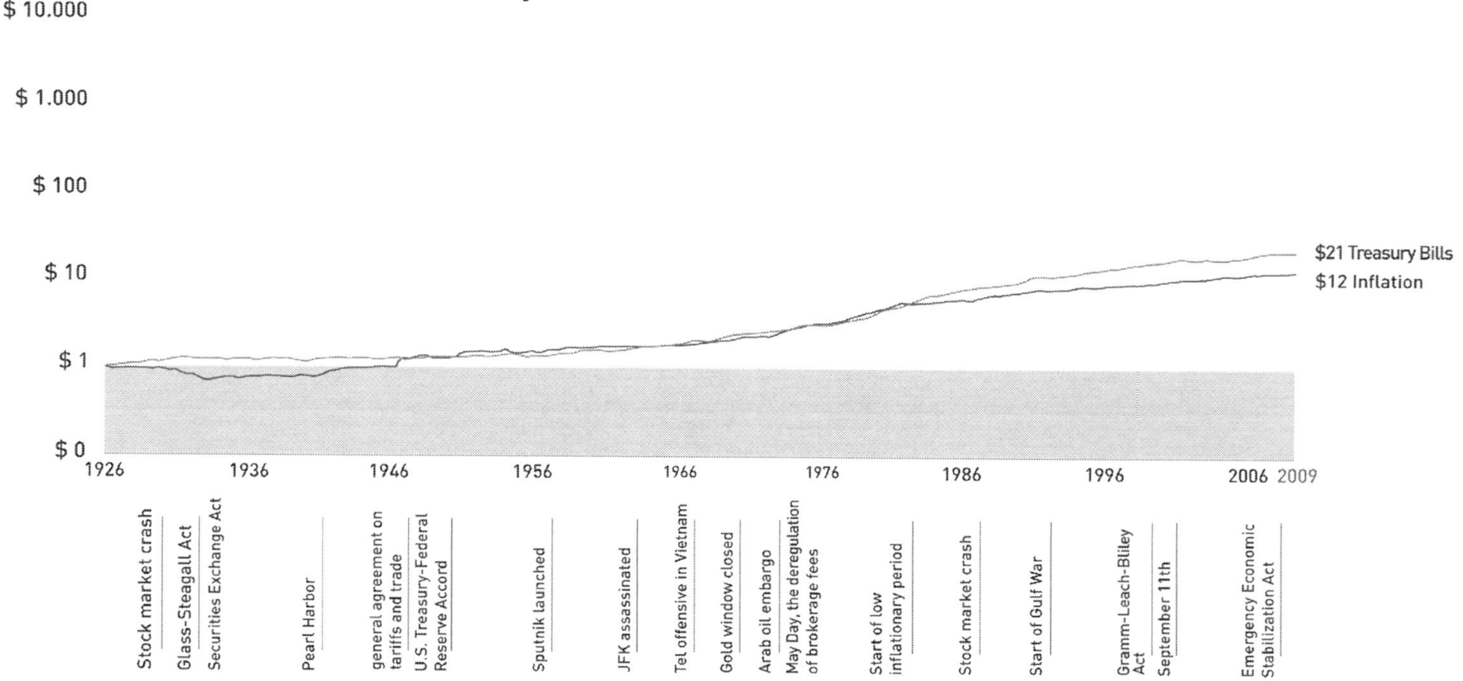

$10.000

$1.000

$100

$10

$1

$0

1926 1936 1946 1956 1966 1976 1986 1996 2006 2009

$21 Treasury Bills

$12 Inflation

Stock market crash

Glass-Steagall Act

Securities Exchange Act

Pearl Harbor

general agreement on tariffs and trade

U.S. Treasury-Federal Reserve Accord

Sputnik launched

JFK assassinated

Tet offensive in Vietnam

Gold window closed

Arab oil embargo

May Day, the deregulation of brokerage fees

Start of low inflationary period

Stock market crash

Start of Gulf War

Gramm-Leach-Bliley Act

September 11th

Emergency Economic Stabilization Act

CRSP data provided by the Center for Research in Security Prices, University of Chicago. The S&P data are provided by Standard & Poor's Index Services Group.US long-term bonds, bills, inflation, income factor data © Stocks, Bonds, Bills, and Inflation Yearbook TM , Ibbotson Associates, Chicago (annually updated work by Roger G. Ibbotson and Rex A. Sinquefield).

Creating value: stocks

L et's go back to the graph on inflation and U.S. government bonds, and add a line showing the market movement of the S&P 500—the 500 biggest U.S. companies—over the same eighty-three-year period.

Reflecting events between 1926 and 2009, the curve reveals some great successes and some dramatic failures. Some companies drop out of the S&P 500 while others join it, but despite bankruptcies, buybacks, and market crashes, the line steadily rises, so that $1 in 1926 turns into $2,592 today. In other words, a million dollars invested in 1926 would be worth $2.592 billion in December 2009.

The U.S. small-cap stock index is even more telling: there, $1 grew to $12,231! These small entities are more volatile, of course, but when they succeed, they gain tremendously in value.[119]

Risk and return are related: small companies are riskier than big ones, but they offer greater returns.

119   Steven L. Heston, Geert K. Rousenhorst, and Roberto E. Wessels. "The Structure of International Stock Returns and the Integration of Capital Markets." *Journal of Empirical Finance 2:3* (1995):173-197.

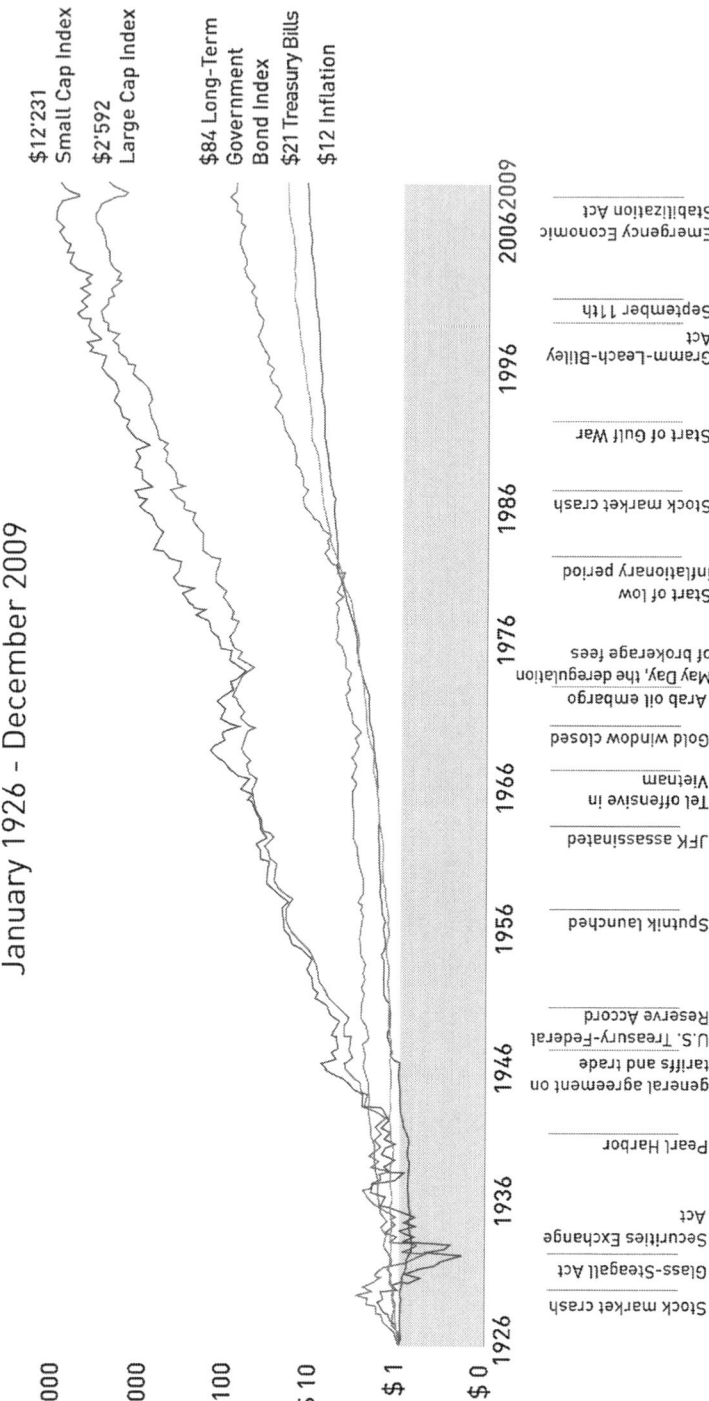

January 1926 - December 2009

$ 10.000
$ 1.000
$ 100
$ 10
$ 1
$ 0

$12'231 Small Cap Index
$2'592 Large Cap Index
$84 Long-Term Government Bond Index
$21 Treasury Bills
$12 Inflation

1926 1936 1946 1956 1966 1976 1986 1996 2006 2009

Stock market crash
Glass-Steagall Act
Securities Exchange Act
Pearl Harbor
general agreement on tariffs and trade
U.S. Treasury-Federal Reserve Accord
Sputnik launched
JFK assassinated
Tet offensive in Vietnam
Gold window closed
Arab oil embargo
May Day, the deregulation of brokerage fees
Start of low inflationary period
Stock market crash
Start of Gulf War
Gramm-Leach-Bliley Act
September 11th
Emergency Economic Stabilization Act

CRSP data provided by the Center for Research in Security Prices, University of Chicago. The S&P data are provided by Standard & Poor's Index Services Group. US long-term bonds, bills, inflation, income factor data © Stocks, Bonds, Bills, and Inflation Yearbook TM , Ibbotson Associates, Chicago (annually updated work by Roger G. Ibbotson and Rex A. Sinquefield).

The impact of compound interest on fees and performance

When an investment pays interest and that interest is reinvested, it produces "compound interest"—interest on interest. This extremely important concept means that a very small percentage difference can have a tremendous long-term impact.

> "When asked what he considered man's greatest discovery, Albert Einstein replied without hesitation: 'Compound interest!'"
>
> **Charles Ellis**
> *Investment Policy*, **1985**

The impact of compound interest on fees:

Let's suppose you have a capital of one million dollars that earns 6.5% a year, and that your banker or manager takes a 1% annual management fee. At the end of thirty years, your million dollars will be worth 5 million dollars.

But now suppose that under the same circumstances the manager charges 3%. At the end of thirty years your million dollars will be worth only 2.8 million dollars—only about half as much!

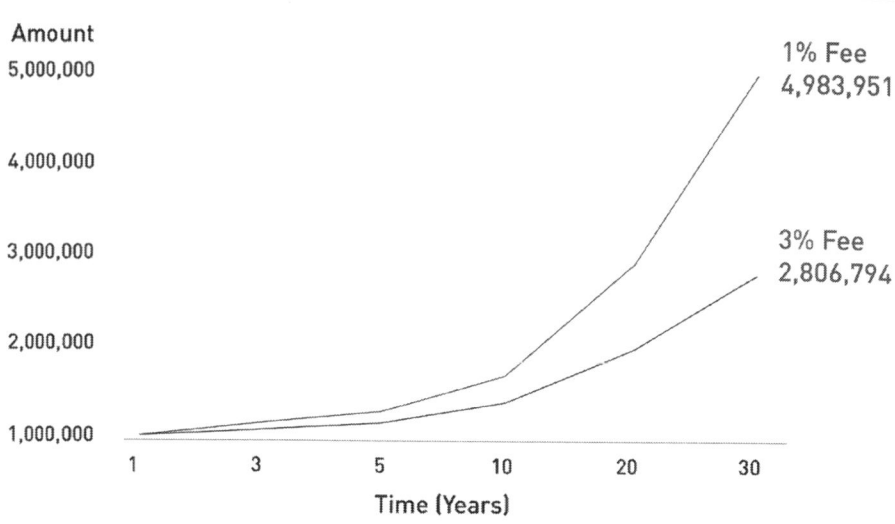

The impact of compound interest on performance:

When compound interest is always reinvested, it creates more value than any other single factor. Take the story of the 1626 sale of Manhattan Island, which the Indians supposedly sold for goods worth $24. That sale has been called the worst deal in history, since the island today is worth an estimated $528 billion.[120] If the Indians had invested their initial capital of $24 and gotten a return of 6% per year, the investment would be worth $118 billion by the end of 2009. But if they had invested the same amount and earned a 6.5% return,[121] the initial $24 would be worth $716 billion! This example shows that a small difference in return (0.5% a year) can have a gigantic impact in the long term ($598 billion).

---

120   Jhoanna S. Robledo. "Because we wouldn't trade a patch of grass for $528,783,552,000." http://nymag.com/nymetro/news/reasonstoloveny/15362, December 18, 2005.
121   By comparison, a portfolio invested 50% in stocks and 50% in bonds for the last eighty years would have produced an average annual return of about 8%.

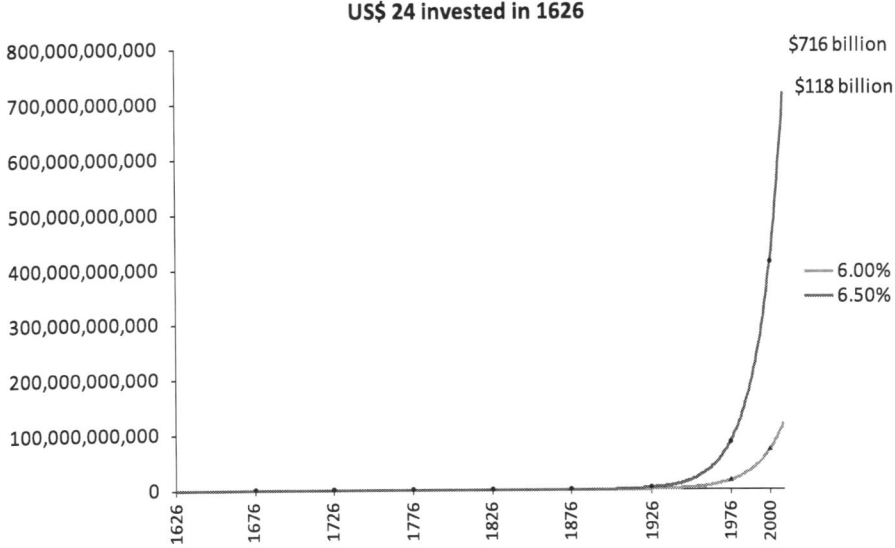

US$ 24 invested in 1626

"The secret of getting rich slowly (but surely) is the miracle of compound interest — One dollar invested in stocks since 1802 would have accumulated to almost $7 million by the end of 2002"

Burton Malkiel
A Random Walk Down Wall Street, **1973**

The effect of asset allocation on portfolio performance

Mathematical and statistical methods are used to prove the connection between various factors. They show, for instance, that the variations of temperature in Switzerland are largely explained by the seasons and the cycles of day and night.

The same methods can explain the factors behind investment performance. Studies on the subject[122] reveal that by far the biggest factor in a portfolio's performance (about 90%) is the level of the risk chosen. In other words, how many fixed income assets are held compared to riskier ones.

Determinants of Portfolio Performance

Over 90 % of portfolio performance is determined by the asset allocation decision.

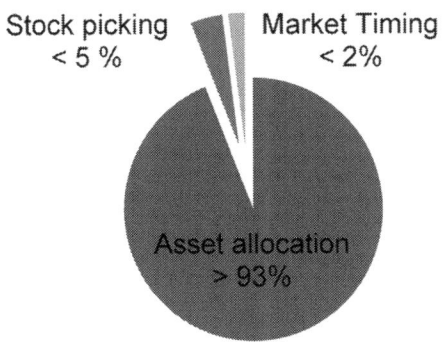

Stock picking
< 5 %

Market Timing
< 2%

Asset allocation
> 93%

122   Gary P. Brinson, L. Randolph Hood, and Gilbert L. Beebower. "Determinants of Portfolio Performance." *Financial Analysts Journal*, July-August 1986. Follow-up study, "Revisiting Determinants of Portfolio Performance: An Update" 1990 Working Paper, 1986, 1990

Critics of this conclusion claim that tactical allocation (market timing)[123] is responsible for performance, but they are mistaken. Studies clearly prove that long-term strategic allocation is the determining factor, for instance in the choice between a balanced or a conservative portfolio.

---

123   See technical note, "Market timing." , page 85

Unnecessary risks

A risk is considered "unnecessary" if it rewards a few lucky people but costs average investors much more than it offers. In some cases the risk yields nothing and can even lead to a net loss. The risks described below fall into this category.

- **The risk of fraud**: There are many unfortunate examples of this, and new cases pop up every year. In spite of legislation and controls put in place by the authorities,[124] reports of fraud persist in the financial pages.
- **The risk of custodian bankruptcy** (bank failure): If liquid assets are carried on a bank's balance sheet or in fiduciary deposits, bankruptcy can lead to the total loss of these assets.[125]
- **Management risk**: the risk that the manager will choose bad investments.
- **Forex risk**: An investment made in a foreign currency risks depreciation of the investment currency relative to the reference currency.
- **Interest rate risk**: The longer the investment term, the greater the risk that the value will be eroded by high inflation.[126]
- **Liquidity risk:** Some investments may be frozen for months. This means that the owners of the funds must wait to recover their money.

---

124   Today, and especially since the discovery of the Madoff affair, many countries have set up mechanisms to regulate funds. In Europe, for example, UCITS III requires that funds be structured in a way that protects investors from fraud.

125   See technical note, "Why it's risky to hold cash?" , page 115

126   See technical note, "Short term government bonds in your country's currency." , page 119

- **Company bankruptcy risk**: If the company that issued the stock in the account goes bankrupt (Swissair, for example) the money invested will be lost.[127]

All these risks can be eliminated. So why run them, especially when you know their potential cost?

> "Index funds eliminate the risks of individual stocks, market sectors, and manager selection. Only stock market risk remains."
>
> **John C. Bogle**
> *The Little Book of Common Sense Investing,* 2007

---

127   This risk also exists in a passive portfolio, but since it holds stocks in thousands of companies, the impact of a bankruptcy is negligible (hence the importance of diversification).

Inflation and volatility

Inflation

Inflation refers to increases in the cost of living. What you could once buy for 1 dollar costs 2, 5, or 10 dollars today. If you keep a banknote in your wallet for ten years, its face value is protected, but it loses purchasing power because of the general rise in prices. Inflation is a persistent, inevitable phenomenon. You can do nothing about it except resign yourself philosophically and stop worrying.

Volatility

Volatility is the measure of an investment's value swings. It is a parameter that quantifies a financial asset's risk. When an investment has high volatility, you might earn large gains, but you also risk large losses.

Market volatility mainly depends on three factors:[128]

- The market itself: Returns from stocks are higher than fixed yields (bonds).
- Market capitalization: Returns from small companies are higher than those of big companies (the small-cap effect).

128
- Eugene F. Fama & Kenneth R. French. "Common Risk Factors in the Returns on Stocks and Bonds." *Journal of Financial Economics*, 33:1 (1993),3-56.
- Eugene F. Fama & Kenneth R. French. "The Cross-Section of Expected Stock Returns." *Journal of Finance,* 47:2 (1992), 427-465.
- Steven L Heston, Geert K., Rousenhorst, and Roberto E., Wessels. "The Structure of International Stock Returns and the Integration of Capital Markets." *Journal of Empirical Finance* 2:3 (1995).

- Returns from value companies, which trade at low prices, are higher than those of growth stocks (the value-cap effect).

The three risks listed above are useful and can be managed. They are the only ones that produce consistent results, provided the investor is patient.

The necessary compromise[129]

Inflation and volatility are the only two risks that can't be eliminated from a portfolio.

Because of their higher returns, stocks offer long-term protection against inflation. Because of their safety, bonds protect against the volatility of stocks but are vulnerable to inflation.

So investors must decide whether they want to guard against:

- market volatility, in which case they should buy a larger proportion of bonds but recognize that they are more exposed to the risk of inflation, or
- inflation, in which case they should invest in a larger proportion of stocks, and thereby expose themselves to price fluctuation (volatility).

---

129   See technical note, "Stock and bonds." , page 111

Passive management: 5% extra performance

Year after year, the market outperforms the average active investor,[130] for two reasons:

- **Expenses**: On average, active management costs twice as much as passive management.[131]
- **The cost of error:** Bad management decisions produce lost opportunity costs. For example, by buying a fund or a traded asset that underperforms, the investor passes up the chance to earn the market's average return.

Many studies[132] have shown that compared to the market, active management costs the investor between 3% and 6% per year.

Take the study quoted by *The Economist* in February 2008. It compared the performance of the S&P 500—the index consisting of the 500 biggest U.S. companies—with that of stock funds trying to beat the S&P 500 index.

---

130 See technical note, "Few managers beat the markets." , page 93

131

– Kenneth R. French, "The Cost of Active Investing." *Journal of Finance*, http://ssrn.com/abstract=1105775, April 2008.

– This calls for an overall calculation that takes into consideration not only management fees, but also transaction, agent, and fund fees.

132

– Andy Baker. "Money for old hope." *Special Report from The Economist*, 28.02.2008.

– Jonathan Clements, "Only Fools Fall in... Managed funds?" *Wall Street Journal*, 15.09.2002.

– Pat Regnier. "Can you outsmart the markets?" *Fortune Magazine*, 21.12.2009.

– Standard & Poor's. "Standard & Poor's Indices Versus Active Funds Scorecard, Year End 2008." http://www.standardandpoors.com/indices/spiva/en/us, 20.04.2009.

– Jason Zweig. "Why so many investors keep fooling themselves?" *Wall Street Journal*, 16.01.2010.

From 1980 to 2005, the S&P 500 rose an average of 12.3% per year. But an investor who bought a stock fund would have earned only 7.3% a year. Compounded over a long period, that 5% annual difference would have had a catastrophic effect on a portfolio's performance.[133]

In fact, for each $1 million invested, the average investor would only receive $5.4 million after 25 years, whereas if he had simply held all the stocks that make up the S&P 500, he would earn $16.1 million. This represents a lost opportunity to earn more than $10 million for each $1 million invested!

Economist.com Feb 28th, 2008

"Over the 25 years from 1980 to 2005, the S&P500 index returned an average of 12.3% a year [...] the average investor earned just 7.3%"

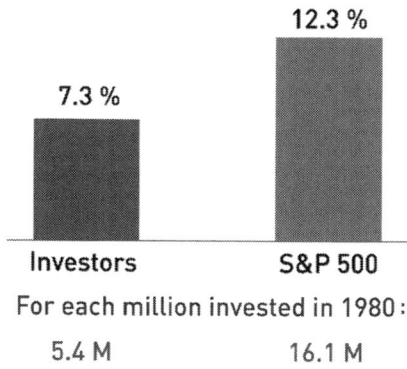

For each million invested in 1980:

5.4 M   16.1 M

---

133   See technical note, "The impact of compound interest on fees and performance." , page 125

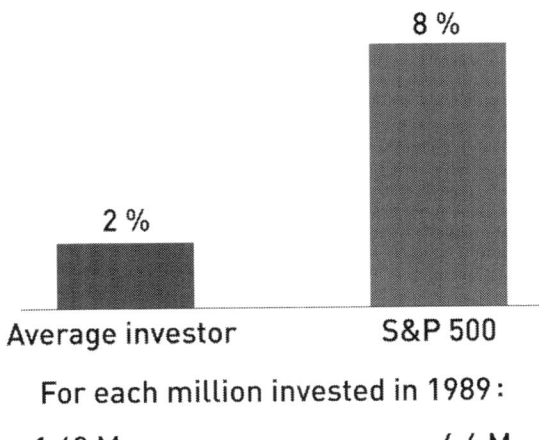

21 December, 2009

"From 1989 through 2008, the S&P500 gained a bit more than 8% a year, but the average investor earned less than 2% [...]"

For each million invested in 1989:

Emotional finance

How do your emotions affect your investments?

People are capable of making rational decisions, but when their financial worth is involved, rationality often disappears and emotions take over. It is not easy to be a rational investor in the face of an erratic, unpredictable market.

To stay calm when the market goes crazy, you should:

- Risk only assets that you don't need in order to pay your bills.
- Develop an investment strategy based on a well-defined financial plan.[134]
- Change that plan only if your personal situation requires it. Don't let external events affect your goals!

---

134 See technical note, "Setting your goals and creating a financial plan." , page 103

- Do not allow yourself to be influenced by media noise or by the wild behavior of markets.
- Remember that even experts can't predict stock price movements.
- Give up the idea of beating the market.

Index management vs. passive management

Many people—even financial professionals—tend to confuse these two management techniques. Both approaches were born in the 1970s, with the appearance of the first studies showing that on average, markets outperform active managers.

Portfolio management can be divided into three main categories: active management (stock picking, etc.), index management, and passive management.

<u>Index management:</u>

- Eliminates stock picking and manager selection but uses market timing.[135] This technique still involves forecasting and therefore a risk of error.
- Uses index funds, index trackers, or exchange traded funds (ETFs) designed to mimic precisely the movement of a specific index. Investments are made in most of the stocks that make up an index, or by artificially replicating it. This approach focuses on managing the so-called tracking error, which is the gap between the fund and the reference index:
  - Indexes were created for measurement, not for investment.
  - Indexes tend to favor expensive stocks.
  - Most indexes include only part of the class of assets they are supposed to represent. For example an MSCI World index tracker holds only about 1,700 out of 75,000 securi-

135   See technical notes, "stock-picking," "market timing," and "manager selection.", pages 83, 85 and 87

ties—just 2.3% of what is available.

- Index funds are designed to stay close to the reference index, which forces them to sell and buy at the same time as
everyone else. As a result, they are hostage to a pattern of
buy high – sell low, while also increasing transaction fees.
- Index funds may suffer from large premiums or discounts.
- Index funds are actively traded, which increases costs for
static investors.
- Many index funds are sold through brokers and financial
advisors, which can be expensive.
- Index fund promoters tend to keep a large share of the
revenue earned from securities lending.

Note: It is hard to choose among these instruments because there
are now thousands of index funds of all sorts. Despite their image of
a product that is simple and low risk, the growth and proliferation of
index funds calls for careful analysis of the funds, in particular of how
they are constructed, their strategies, and their compensation.

Passive management:

- Eliminates stock picking and manager selection.
- Rejects market timing. Passive managers don't rely on forecasts,
recognizing that there is no way to know when markets will rise
or fall. They provide "buy and hold" management. Once the
money is invested, the passive manager patiently waits for the
market to produce the expected returns. There is no worry and
no decisions to be made, because the investor remains invested
no matter what happens. When the market drops, he has a ring-
side seat for its recovery.
- Uses portfolio rebalancing. This allows the manager to buy low
and sell high.
- Works to minimize the dramatic impact of management and
transaction fees on a portfolio's performance. With this in mind,
the passive manager chooses and uses only passively managed
funds with a low total expense ratio (TER).[136] A passive portfolio
should cost no more than 1.5% per year, including all expenses,
such as management, agent, bank, transaction, and fund fees.

---

136   TER is total expense ratio, a measure of how much a fund costs the client per year.

- Eliminates the risk of error because all decisions are fact-based; emotional and predictive factors are ignored.
- Uses passive funds and avoids using index funds, trackers, or ETFs.

ADVANTAGES AND DISADVANTAGES OF THE THREE KINDS OF MANAGEMENT

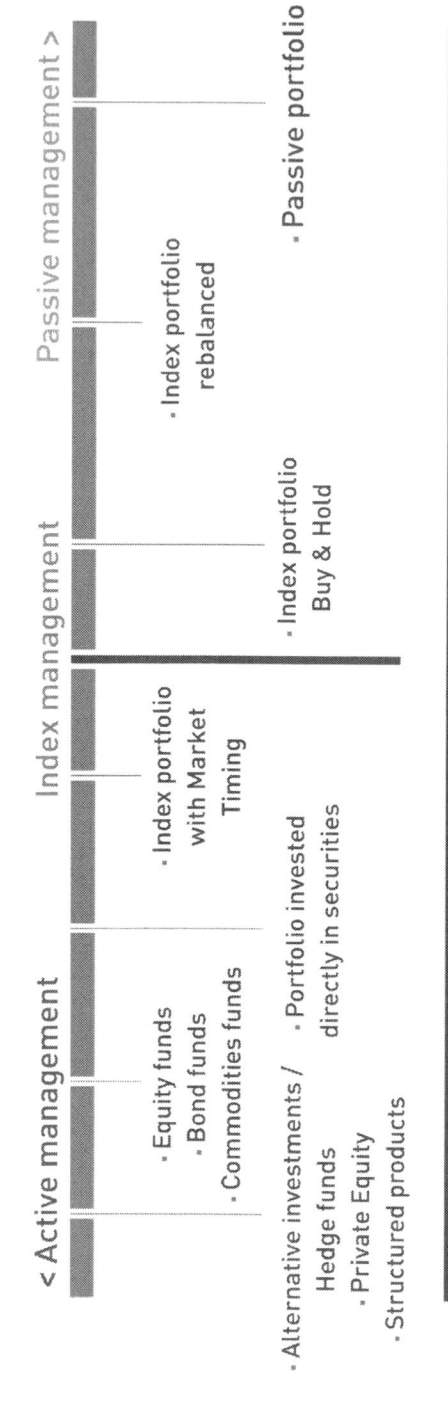

< Active management   Index management   Passive management >

· Equity funds
· Bond funds
· Commodities funds

· Index portfolio
  with Market
  Timing

· Index portfolio
  Buy & Hold

· Index portfolio
  rebalanced

· Passive portfolio

· Alternative investments /   · Portfolio invested
  Hedge funds   directly in securities
· Private Equity
· Structured products

Profitability limit for non fee only advisors (banks, commission based asset managers & advisors, etc)

+ Transparency
+ Liquidity
+ Performance
+ Peace of mind

+ Forecast
+ Risk of mistake
+ Fees
+ Gambling appeal

The history of passive management

Passive management is rooted in academic research and based on facts. Its methods result from observing markets and drawing conclusions from these observations.

In the 1950s, the growth in computing power allowed economists to gather and record all the available data about trading markets. At the same time, the University of Chicago was making notable progress in developing various investment models. In 1964 William Sharpe developed the Capital Asset Pricing Model (CAPM).[137] This model is the backbone of modern capital market theory, and it proves that stock market price movements are unpredictable. In 1965 Paul Samuelson suggested that the best estimate of the inherent value of a stock was the price set by the market itself at every minute of the day.[138] No other estimate could be more accurate than the price set by the stock's buyers and sellers. That same year, Eugene Fama demonstrated that markets are efficient enough to allow all new information to be precisely and immediately reflected in the price of each stock.[139]

In 1968, Michael Jensen completed the first large-scale study of performance by examining 115 U.S. stock funds between 1945 and 1964. His conclusion was simple: no fund manager had been able to predict the price of stocks well enough to allow his fund to outperform the market for any reason besides pure chance.[140]

---

137   William Sharpe. "Capital asset prices: a theory of market equilibrium under conditions of risk." *Journal of Finance* 19:3 (1964): 425-442.
138   Paul Samuelson. "Proof that Properly Anticipated Prices Fluctuate Randomly." *Industrial Management Review* (1965): 41.
139   Eugene F. Fama. Ph.D. dissertation, "The Behavior of Stock Market Prices." *Journal of Business*, January 1965.
140   Michael Jensen. "The Performance of Mutual Funds in the Period 1945-1965." *Journal of Finance* 23:2 (1967).

In 1973, Burton Malkiel presented this academic research to the general public in his classic book, *A Random Walk Down Wall Street*. In it, he showed that most mutual funds don't beat the market as measured by the index. Fund managers retorted that in any case it was impossible to buy an index—to which Malkiel responded that it was high time for that to change!

That same year, John McQuown and David Booth at Wells Fargo and Rex Sinquefield at the American National Bank of Chicago created the first funds that matched the Standard & Poor's 500 Index. The funds were reserved for institutional clients.

In 1974, John Bogle founded The Vanguard Group and began offering passive funds. (The group has since become the biggest mutual fund stock manager in the United States for private and institutional investors.) In December 1975, Bogle launched his first index fund, drawing inspiration from three papers that supported his thesis research: "Challenge to Judgment," by Paul Samuelson; "The Loser's Game," by Charles Ellis; and "Some Kinds of Mutual Funds Make Sense," by Al Ehrbar.

Assets under Vanguard management were relatively limited in the beginning (about $11 million), but they passed the $100 billion level in 1999. The following year Vanguard overtook the Magellan Fund to become one of the largest funds in the world.

The efficient market hypothesis

The efficient market hypothesis (EMH)[141] asserts that at any given moment the price of a traded asset already reflects all available information, and that this price will instantly change to reflect new information. The future movement of the price will depend on new data, which is impossible to predict and will be available to everyone at the same time.

Critics of the EMH theory argue that markets are irrational. They note that prices are sometimes abnormally low or high—the 1999 technology bubble is an example. They are correct and the EMH supports them. Markets are indeed often irrational. The theory doesn't,

> "There is no other proposition in economics that has more solid empirical evidence supporting it than the Efficient Market Hypothesis...In the literature of finance, accounting, and the economics of uncertainty, the EMH is accepted as a fact of life."
>
> Micheal C. Jensen
> "Some Anomalous Evidence Regarding Market Efficiency,"
> Journal of Financial Economics, 1978

141
– Eugene F. Fama. "Efficient Capital Markets: A Review of Theory and Empirical Work." *Journal of Finance* 25:2 (1970): 383-417.
– Eugene F. Fama. "The Behavior of Stock Market Prices." *Journal of Business* 38 (1965) : 34-105.
– Jeremy J. Siegel. "Efficient Market Theory and the Crisis." *Wall Street Journal,* 27.10.2009.

however, claim that markets are rational or that the prices are fair. EMH explains that irrationalities are hard to detect, and when discovered they instantly disappear. Consequently, they don't allow the investor to benefit enough to produce extraordinary returns.

The implications of the efficient market hypothesis are important. An investor buys (or sells) a traded asset on the assumption that its intrinsic value is higher (or lower) than its price, and hopes to benefit from the spread. But since nobody can know in advance what changes will take place in the future....

About the Authors

For several decades, Alexandre Arnbäck and Trevor Pavitt worked as bankers in private and international banks. They grew uncomfortable with having to sell their customers more and more products, increasing profitability for the bank but often disappointing investors. Thus, they decided to join forces in finding the best solution for their customers.

They founded Passive Management SA, an independent wealth planning firm based in Geneva, to help investors achieve their most important goals. They focus on understanding their clients' needs and work with a team of experts to create a robust plan—one that integrates all aspects of wealth management, from tax and inheritance planning to asset protection and charitable donations.

In this book, they break down the complexities of the financial market so that investors can learn to control and protect their own portfolios.

Alexandre Arnbäck

Thanks to his professional and family background, Alexandre Arnbäck is best able to help women who have the responsibility of family wealth and who seek financial stability to ensure that they can provide for their families with complete peace of mind.

Alexandre earned his master of business administration from ESADE Business School in Barcelona and Duke University. He started his career as head of analytical accounting before joining the private bank of Lombard Odier Darier Hentsch & Cie. He worked as a private banker for eight years between Geneva and the Bahamas.

Trevor Pavitt

Trevor Pavitt leverages his 20 years of banking experience to help people faced with financial transitions. His expertise enables them to navigate the financial complexities that come with retirement, marriage or divorce, sale of a business or of real estate, and the receipt of a bonus or an inheritance.

Trevor graduated from the University of Geneva with a degree in business. He earned his stockbroker license from the Securities and Exchange Commission in New York and studied management at INSEAD in Paris. He worked with Trade Development Bank, Boston Trust & Deposit Company, American Express Bank, KPMG, and Digital before serving as director of the Iberia and Latin America team with Barclays Wealth in Geneva.

Bibliography

Books

- Adam Smith, *An Inquiry into the Nature and Causes of the Wealth of Nations*, 1776.
- Alfred Marshall. *Principles of Economics*, 8th ed. New York: Cosimo Inc., 2009.
- Anil Gaba, Robin Hogarth, and Spyros Makridakis. *Dance with Chance.* Oxford: Oneworld Publications, 2009.
- Burton G. Malkiel. *A Random Walk Down Wall Street*. New York: W.W. Norton & Company Inc., 2007.
- Charles D. Ellis. *Winning the Loser's Game, Timeless Strategies for Successful Investing*. New York: McGraw Hill, 2002.
- Christopher R. Balke and Matthew Morey. "Morningstar Ratings and Mutual Fund Performance." *Fordham University's Graduate School of Business*. December 22, 1999.
- Gary Belsky and Thomas Gilovich. *Why Smart People Make Big Money Mistakes, and How to Correct Them*. New York: Simon & Schuster, 1999.
- Harry M. Markowitz. *Portfolio Selection*: *Efficient Diversification of Investments*. New York: John Wiley & Sons, Inc., 1959.
- Jeremy J. Siegel. *Stocks for the Long Run.* New York: McGraw-Hill, 1998.
- John C. Bogle. *Common Sense on Mutual Funds.* Hoboken, NJ: John Wiley & Sons, Inc., 2010.
- John C. Bogle. *The Little Book of Common Sense Investing.* Hoboken, NJ: John Wiley & Sons Inc., 2007.
- John Bowen, Jr. and Daniel C Goldie. *The Prudent Investor's Guide to Beating Wall Street at Its Own Game.* Kindle Edition, 1998.

- Larry E. Swedroe. *The Only Guide to a Winning Investment Strategy You'll Ever Need.* New York: Truman Talley Books/ Dutton, 1998.
- Larry E. Swedroe. *What Wall Street Doesn't Want You to Know.* New York: Truman Talley Books/Dutton, 2001.
- Richard A. Ferri. *All About Asset Allocation.* New York: McGraw-Hill, 2006.
- Richard A. Ferri. *All About Index Funds.* New York: McGraw-Hill, 2002.
- Richard A. Ferri. *The ETF Book, All You Need to Know About Exchange-Traded Funds.* Hoboken, NJ: John Wiley & Sons Inc., 2007.
- Ron Ross, Ph.D. *The Unbeatable Market, Taking the Indexing Path to Financial Peace of Mind.* Eureka, CA: Optimum Press, 2002.
- Sasha Gironde. *La Neuroéconomie, Comment le cerveau gère mes intérêts.* Paris: Edition Plon, 2008.
- Sidney Homer. *A History of Interest Rates.* New Brunswick, NJ: Rutgers University Press, 1963.
- Smith Barney Consulting Group. *Why Top Performance Is a Poor Indicator of Future Performance.* 1997.
- Tim Hale. *Smarter Investing: Simpler Decisions for Better Results,* 2nd ed. Harlow, U.K.: Pearson Education Ltd, 2009.
- William Berstein. *The Intelligent Asset Allocator.* New York: McGraw Hill, 2001.
- William A. Sherden. *The Fortune Sellers.* New York: John Wiley & Sons, Inc., 1998.
- William Bernstein. *The Four Pillars of Investing: Lessons for Building a Winning Portfolio.* New York: McGraw Hill, 2002.

Articles

- AFP. "La crise va empirer selon DSK. " *Le Figaro.* 12.12.2008.
- Alfred Cowles III, "Can Stock Market Forecasters Forecast?", *Econometria* 1:3 (July 1933).
- Andy Baker. *The Economist,* Special Report "Money for Old Hope." 01.03.2008.
- Anna Robaton. "FRC Study Raps Morningstar Ratings: All-Star Battle Over Performance." *Investment News.* 29.03.1999.

- Brad M. Barber. Terrance Odean, and Lu Zheng. "Out of Sight, Out of Mind: The Effects of Expenses on Mutual Fund Flows." *Journal of Business* 78 (2005).
- Christian Nolterieke. "Cut the Costs of Wealth Management." 28.05.2009. http://www.myprivatebanking.com/report/wealth-guide-2
- Claire Gatinois and Anne Michel. "Société Générale: six questions sur une fraude." *Le Monde*, 26.01.2008.
- DALBAR Study "Shows Market Timers Lose Their Money." press release, April 2004.
- D. Kahnemann, E. Higgens, and W. Riepe, W. "Aspects of Investor Psychology." *Journal of Portfolio Management* 24:4 (1998).
- David Bogoslaw. "Retirement: Goal-Based Investing Gains Traction." *Bloomberg Businessweek.* 18.08.2009.
- David Booth and Eugene F. Fama, "Diversification Returns and Asset Contributions." *Financial Analysts Journal.* May/June 1992.
- Ellen Langer. "The Illusion of Control." Journal of Personality and Social Psychology 32:2 (1975).
- Eugene F. Fama & Kenneth R. French. "Common Risk Factors in the Returns on Stocks and Bonds." *Journal of Financial Economics* 33 :1 (1993)
- Eugene F. Fama and Kenneth R. French, "Luck versus Skill in the Cross Section of Mutual Fund Returns." *Journal of Finance* (December 2009)
- Eugene F. Fama and Kenneth R. French, "The Cross-Section of Expected Stock Returns." *Journal of Finance* 47 (1992).
- Eugene F. Fama and Kenneth R. French, "The Cross-Section of Expected Stock Returns." *Journal of Finance*, December 1998
- Eugene F. Fama and Kenneth R. French, "Value versus Growth: The International Evidence." *Journal of Finance*, December 1998
- Eugene F. Fama, "Efficient Capital Markets: A Review of Theory and Empirical Work." *Journal of Finance* 25:2 (1970).
- Eugene F. Fama, Ph.D dissertation. "The Behavior of Stock Market Prices." *The Journal of Business* (January 1965)
- Gary P. Brinson, L. Randolph Hood, and Gilbert L. Beebower. "Determinants of Portfolio Performance." *Financial Analysts Journal*, July-August 1986, Follow-up study, "Revisiting

Determinants of Portfolio Performance: An Update" 1990 Working Paper, 1986, 1990.

- Gregory Zuckerman. "Love'em! Hate'em!" *The Wall Street Journal*. 07.02.2005.
- Hilary Osborne. "Financial advisers' commission to cease, says FSA." *guardian.co.uk,* 26.03.2010.
- Ian Cowie. "Warren Buffet "fund" illustrates rip off management charges." *Daily Telegraph*. 29.09.2010.
- Interview of John Bogle by Heather Bell "Active vs. Passive." *Journal of Indexes*. March/April 2009.
- Interview of Warren Buffett by Julia Boorstin, "The Best Advice I Ever Got." *Fortune Magazine*. 21.03.2005.
- James K. Glassman. "Attempts to Time the Market Always Leave the Investor Out of Sync." *New York Times*. 12.11.2001.
- James L. Davis. "Mutual Fund Performance and Manager Style." *Financial Analyst Journal* 57:1 (2001).
- Jason Zweig. "Why Many Investors Keep Fooling Themselves." *Wall Street Journal*. 16.01.2010.
- Jean-Claude Péclet. "Comment payer mon banquier?" *Le Temps*. 02.02.2009.
- Jeremy J. Siegel. "Efficient Market Theory and the Crisis." *The Wall Street Journal*. 27.10.2009.
- Jhoanna S. Robledo. "Because we wouldn't trade a patch of grass for $528,783,552,000." http://nymag.com/nymetro/news/reasonstoloveny/15362, December 18, 2005.
- John Arlidge. "I'm Doing God's Work: Meet Mister Goldman Sachs." *Sunday Times*. 08.11.2009.
- Jonathan Clements. "Only Fools Fall in...Managed Funds?" *Wall Street Journal*. 15.09.2002.
- Kenneth R. French, "The Cost of Active Investing." *Journal of Finance*, http://ssrn.com/abstract=1105775, April 2008.
- Mark Grinblatt and Sheridan Titman. "The Impact of Performance-based Fees on Pension Fund Management." Finance Working Paper, Anderson Graduate School of Management, University of California at Los Angeles, rev. February 1987.
- Mark Hulbert. "Can You Beat the Market? It's a $100 Billion Question." *New York Times,* 09.03.2008.

- Michael Jensen. "The Performance of Mutual Funds in the Period 1945–1964."*Journal of Finance* 23:2 (1967).
- Pat Regnier. "Can You Outsmart the Market?" *Fortune 2010 Investor's Guide*, 11.12.2009.
- Paul A. Samuelson. "Proof That Properly Anticipated Prices Fluctuate Randomly." *Industrial Management Review* 6:2 (1965).
- Philip Coggan. *The Economist*, Special Report "Money for Old Hope." 01.03.2008.
- Pierre Novello. "Le point sur les commissions d'émission et les rétrocessions." *Le Temps*, 03.02.2010.
- Prof. L. Barras, O. Scaillet, and R. Wermers, Swiss Finance Institute. "False Discoveries in Mutual Fund Performance: Measuring Luck in Estimated Alphas." in *Research Paper Series* N°08-18, 2008.
- Stephen J. Brown, William N. Goetzmann, and Liang Bing. "Fees on Fees in Funds of Funds." *Journal of Investment Management* 2, 2004.
- Steven L. Heston, Geert K. Rousenhorst, and Roberto E. Wessels. "The Structure of International Stock Returns and the Integration of Capital Markets," *Journal of Empirical Finance 2:3* (1995).
- Sylvain Cypel. "Comment 'Bernie' les a tous bernés." Le Monde, 16.12.2008.
- Warren Giles. "Rich Pumped for Fees in Banking Conflict of Interest." *Business Week*, 24.03.2010.
- William F. Sharpe. "Capital Asset Prices: A Theory of Market Equilibrium Under Conditions of Risk." *Journal of Finance* 19:3 (1964).
- William F. Sharpe. "The Arithmetic of Active Management." *Financial Analysts Journal* 47:1 (1991).
- Yves Genier. "L'insatisfaction d'une perte est plus forte que le plaisir d'un gain." *Le Temps*, 29.09.2007.

Internet Web Sites

- Berkshire Hathaway's annual report for 2005http://www.berk-shirehathaway.com/2005ar/2005ar.pdf
- Confédération Suisse, Office fédéral des assurances sociales, communiqué sur les rétrocessions, 08.04.2010 www.bsv.admin.ch/aufsichtbv/02024/02064/index.html?lang=fr
- http://www.longbets.org/362
- http://www.richelieufinance.fr/fr/revueDesMedias/view?id=11
- Ombudsman des banques suisses, "Rendement élevé égale risque élevé", Communiqué of 07.07.2009 http://www.bankingombudsman.ch
- Standard & Poor's "Does Past Performance Matter?" June 2010 http://img.en25.com/Web/StandardandPoors/PersistenceScorecard_June10_Final.pdf
- Standard & Poor's "Standard & Poor's Indices Versus Active Funds Scorecard, Year End 2008." 20.04.2009, http://www.standardandpoors.com/indices/spiva/en/us
- www.bloomberg.com

Television

- Frédéric Goujon, "Et si UBS faisait faillite?" Toutes Taxes Comprises (Swiss television series, TSR 1), 09.03.2009.

17911614R00089

Made in the USA
Lexington, KY
05 October 2012